THE PORNOG-RAPHY OF POWER

BY
LIONEL RUBINOFF

QUADRANGLE BOOKS
CHICAGO

Library of Congress Catalog Card Number: 68-13462

Designed by Lawrence Levy

"The Second Coming" by W. B. Yeats is quoted by permission of The Macmillan Company, New York, The Macmillan Company of Canada Ltd., and Mr. M. B. Yeats.

TO

Aaron, Ingrid, Daniel,

Leah and David

and to

Suzanne

PREFACE

THE CHAPTERS which make up this book were originally prepared for broadcast over the Canadian Broadcasting Corporation radio network in March, April, and May of 1967, as part of the *Ideas* series on "Money and Power." They are presented here, with permission of the C.B.C., under their original title but in a thoroughly revised and expanded form.

Although I must bear total responsibility for both the substance and style of this book, my debt to the many persons who have helped me is deep and widespread. I am indebted, first of all, to my students, who over the years have continuously pressed me to take stands on issues related to the crises of our time. In choosing to accept this challenge I may possibly have made myself a wiser man, but I have also, and perhaps foolishly, made myself vulnerable to attack from those who live by the belief that philosophers should not meddle in affairs that are no business of philosophy but belong rather to experts in the social sciences. But as I have never really accepted this definition of philosophy in the first place, I see no reason for turning it into a self-fulfilling prophecy by conforming to its injunction. To those who insist, however, that philosophy has no practical application to the world and who fear that whenever philosophers depart from their normal routines they are bound to make fools of themselves, I make the following plea: In affairs *de coeur* it is an acknowledged right of the lover to run the risk of making a fool of himself for the sake of his beloved. Why then should not the philosopher, who is, after all, a lover of another kind, be permitted the same folly for the sake of his passion, which is to follow the melody of the *philosophia quaedam perennis* wherever it happens to lead.

Lest the reader think me harsh on those of my colleagues who wish to remain specialists in their fields and thus remain aloof from the great practical and existential issues of the day, let me hasten to add that if not for the integrity and accomplishments of specialists, and if not for the willingness of some specialists to confront issues of a purely technical nature (even if that means adopting an attitude of indifference to the practical world), an enterprise like mine could hardly have matured. And it is especially because of the presence of such philosophers in the world, philosophers who prefer "analysis" to what otherwise might be called "speculation," that the conclusions of a book like this can be safely offered to the public. Whether the world realizes it or not, the specialists have up until now been the guardians of our civilization. I have learned more from my teachers, who were for the most part professional and highly technical philosophers, than I can ever hope to repay; indeed, the world at large will never know its debt to that tradition of philosophy.

And yet in spite of that debt there are times when rebellious children must rise against their fathers and strike off in new directions. I think it is time to break down the barriers of specialization so that the horizons of the mind can be expanded and men can begin once again to experience the infinity that lives within each of them. The life of philosophy is, I believe, particularly suited to this task.

In addition to my students, teachers, and colleagues, I am indebted to the producers and program organizers of *Ideas* (Phyllis Webb, Janet Somerville, and William Young) for inviting me to deliver the lectures which led to the writing of this book. A very special thanks is due the producer, Janet Somerville, who worked with me throughout the series and whose sympathetic and critical responses to my ideas played a great role in the final success of the series.

I would like also to thank various persons who inhabit the vast world outside the Academy and who have indulged me in my foolishness over the years by inviting me to address them on various subjects having to do with the main substance of this book. Their refusal to be mystified by Academic Rhetoric often led me to fresh insights and certainly caused me to reach for a more lucid expression of what I wanted to say. Among the many from whom I have so profited, I am especially indebted to a small group of professional and lay persons who attended a series of discussion groups which I led at Carman's restaurant in Toronto during 1966 and 1967. It was here that I first entertained some of the ideas embodied in this book. As men of the world, deeply involved in the business of making important and practical decisions, they provided a formidable and highly critical audience for my somewhat speculatively conceived ideas of human conduct.

Finally, I owe a debt to my publishers, Quadrangle Books, and especially to Ivan Dee, managing editor, who not only encouraged me to rewrite the lectures for publication but gave much of his own time to the careful editing of the manuscript. His thoughtful and sensitive criticisms and suggestions are responsible for many improvements. A sabbatical leave granted by York University for the summer and fall of 1967, and a grant from the Canada Council, made it possible for me to live for several months in the shadow of Harvard University, in whose libraries the first drafts of my revisions were completed, and in whose atmosphere both my intuitions and my concepts were substantially refined, enriched, and deepened.

LIONEL RUBINOFF

Toronto
April 1968

CONTENTS

THE
PORNOG-
RAPHY
OF
POWER

INTRODUCTION

I.

This book is an attempt to confront the crisis in values which lies at the center of our current social unrest. As such, it falls within the boundaries of a tradition that is today facing eclipse: the tradition of constructing images and myths for men to live by, and of subjecting them to imaginative appraisal and critique. The social sciences currently indulge in denouncing their classical heritage by adopting the logic and methodology of the pure sciences and by pleading the virtue of being a "value-free" inquiry. Under the influence of this rapidly spreading "scientism," [1] social scientists often lose their sensitivity to the absurdity of things—especially as they become the more expert at constructing explanations. They know the causes of order and disorder, and it no longer fills them with outrage that disorder continues to prevail.

By contrast to the so-called value-free approach of the behavioral sciences, my method in this book is "phenomenological." As opposed to the analytical approach of behavioralism, which seeks to *explain* phenomena by reducing them to general laws, phenomenology is a speculative activity which aims at "understanding" (*verstehen*). In particular, it seeks insight into the "human significance" of the structure of social reality. Scientific behavioralism aims to eliminate mystery. But phenomenology, in confronting things as they are, seeks to elaborate on, and to celebrate in, mystery—the mystery of things existing in themselves and for consciousness alone, independent both of their uses and of the stereotypes through which we normally view them. My book is an attempt, then, to encounter a mystery, the mystery and outrage of man's bewildering capacity for evil, and the mystery of his even more bewildering capacity for transcendence.

I am concerned with two central ideas: progress and power, both of which have had a deep and profound influence on the course of Western history. With the idea of progress came the idea of identifying value with pragmatic and hedonistic goals, goals which can be pursued only through the exercise of power. The hedonistic dimensions of the pursuit of power are what make this phenomenon such a potentially dangerous one. But it is dangerous for still another reason. Progress posits a belief in transcendental goals which both direct and supply the sense of history.

But the irony is that the ideology of progress surreptitiously conspires to introduce the very opposite belief, namely, the relativistic notion that truth is whatever happens to satisfy the needs of the moment. And wherever these needs conflict, power is again invoked as the sole arbiter.

Through the corruption of progress ideology, brought on by the very attempt to live up to it, the pursuit of truth is replaced by the quest for power. Power is the chief goal of all progress-oriented societies. The reason for this lies deep in the structure of human nature. To understand the phenomenon of power, then, presupposes an inquiry into the foundations of human nature. Social scientists *qua* scientists are ambivalent as to whether there is any such thing as human nature at all. In this book I assume there is. I offer no empirical evidence in support of this assumption but try rather to compare and construct various myths, images, and models by means of which the idea of human nature can be rendered intelligible. And, in any case, I doubt whether the idea even needs the support of proof and empirical evidence—any more, that is, than do the ideas of "space," "time," "uniformity of nature," "personal identity," and so on. The result of my analysis is an imaginative and speculative conception of the human condition which embraces both man's nature and his environment. Following Sartre, this condition may be called "situation."

By the second idea, power, I mean primarily the controlled expression of aggression, self-assertion, and potency, by either individuals or groups. This phenomenon goes by many names —love, punishment, justice, social control, discipline, war, government, and so on. My underlying assumption, essentially a metaphysical one, is that every human act or phenomenon is an expression of the whole nature of man and proceeds, therefore, from the primordial character of man's being-in-the-world. Man is the being who makes himself by negating himself. As Sartre puts it, in a phrase which I borrow and repeat throughout, "Man is the source of negativity in the world." The primary means of this ambivalent process is power: power over nature, over oneself, over others, and, ultimately, over the gods. Love, for example, may be understood functionally as an expression and satisfaction of needs, or as an institution which binds together a community. But it is also an expression of power, an implicit form of aggression, and a form of self-making. In love I possess the other as an object to be conquered and subdued. At the same time, love is a creative act which transcends aggression. And the *transcendence* of aggression cannot be conceived apart from the *expression* of it. Likewise, punishment is most often discussed in terms of legality, as an instrument of social control. But punishment is also both an implicit assertion of power and aggression, leading to the satisfaction of a desire for revenge, and a way through which the humanity of the offender can be restored. Political and military power can similarly be viewed as ways of resolving the tension between being and nonbeing.

I am therefore concerned, in this book, with the self-destructive potential of power as it affects man's primordial tendency to evil; and with man's inherent capacity to transcend himself through the creative use of the imagination. The main thesis of this book is that the most effective antidote for the performance of evil is the imagination of evil, and that the most viable therapy for the pathological abuse of power is, accordingly, an imaginative critique of power.

2.

In October 1955 the British anthropologist Geoffrey Gorer published in *Encounter* an article entitled "The Pornography of Death." In this article Gorer drew attention to the possibility that the structure of pornography pervades areas other than sex. Pornography, he wrote, is the description of tabooed activities with the purpose of inciting hallucinations or delusions for private enjoyment. Some aspect of human experience is treated as inherently shameful or abhorrent, so that it can never be discussed or referred to openly, and experience of it tends to be clandestine and accompanied by feelings of guilt and unworthiness. The unmentionable aspect of experience then becomes a subject for private fantasy charged with pleasurable guilt or guilty pleasure. And those whose power of fantasy is weak, or whose demand is insatiable, constitute a market for the commercial fantasies of the professional pornographer.

Traditionally, as Gorer points out, pornography has been associated with sexuality. But sex is not the only human taboo. Death and violence suffer the same fate. Gorer argues that the twentieth century has made death its chief taboo, because the religious belief in immortality is fundamentally inconsistent with the facts of natural death. The result is a refusal even to discuss the question of death.[2] But whenever something is so repressed, the result is almost inevitably a proliferation of fantasies connected with it. Hence the taboo on death results in an increase in the representation of death in fantasies. Furthermore, what is thus represented is always grotesque, distorted, exaggerated, ugly, and sadistic. The pornography of death thus appears through the representation of violence in detective stories, thrillers, war stories, and horror comics.

There is, in other words, a clear-cut parallel between the fantasies which titillate our curiosity about the mystery of sex and those which titillate us about death. In both types of fantasy, the emotions which are typically associated with the acts, such as love and grief, are paid little or no attention, while the purely sensuous dimensions are enhanced to the limits of language. Both types of fantasy are completely unrealistic, for they ignore all physical, social, or legal limitations, and both have as their goal the inducement of hallucination within the reader or viewer.

Just as Gorer has explained the pornography of death, so one could similarly approach other phenomena, such as power and morality. Just as the repression of sex by an overly rationalistic society produces pathological and irrational responses, in the form of sexual fantasies, and the repression of death produces fantasies of violence, so the repression of the irrationality of power and morality produces similar results. Gorer follows tradition in regarding fantasy as the chief way of dealing with repression. Fantasy functions as a substitute form of gratification which corrupts the imagination. I would contend, however, that a depraved imagination almost invariably leads to depraved behavior. In addition to fantasy, in other words, the imagination has access to action as well, so that it is possible for one to *act out* one's repressions. The fact that one also indulges in fantasy does not eliminate or even weaken the possibility of action.

Finally, it is typical of all such behavior that one represents one's action as other than what it is. Thus power, which is intrinsically an expression of irrationality (in the same sense that sex is an expression of irrationality), is represented as something else, as expediency, or as a necessary means to an end (in much the same way that sex is represented as a mere instrument of reproduction). Hence, just as the repression of sex leads to sexual fantasies and sexual perversions, so the repression of the irrationality of power leads not only to the *fantasy* of power but also to the corrupt behavior which is the *exercise of power*.

Modern man has finally discovered, in a profound and disturbing way, an alarming discrepancy between his self-image (which represents him as basically rational and humane) and his actual behavior, which is characteristically irrational. This discovery parallels the experience of Victorian man, who found the pleasures of sex to be inconsistent with the image of it as a purely biological function. The result, in the latter case, was that sexual pleasure became a subject of taboo. (One could discuss the biology and sociology of sex but not the aesthetics of sex.) The same mechanism has operated with respect to death. In much the same way, mid-twentieth-century man resolves his anxiety over the tension between his rationalism and his irrationalism by repressing the latter and intensifying his rationalism.

My point, in other words, is that the repression of man's demonic nature leads inevitably to a search for substitute forms of gratification not only in fantasies but also in direct experiences, such as the behavior of nihilism and violence— although the latter is often represented as essentially rational in character, as useful or expedient. In fact, this behavior is nothing more than a devious route to the unconscious origins of irrationality, a condition which is one of the chief sources of the pornographic character of our behavior. The most potent instrument through which the self asserts itself is power. But when the self is taken over entirely by the irrational, power ceases to be an instrument and becomes a substitute form of gratification. It becomes a self-stimulating and self-reinforcing end. And just as the fantasy form of pornography is typically grotesque, exaggerated, and sadistic, so pornographic action and behavior take on analogous characteristics.

No one willingly admits that his intentions are dishonorable, and one can always convince himself that he is really doing something else. (Seduction is called education, cruelty becomes learning through negative reinforcement, and so on.) For this reason pornography is hard to identify. Whether we employ power and wage war for the sole purpose of defense, or as an instrument of progress, or else for the sheer satisfaction it brings, there is little or no difference in the external makeup of our behavior. In each case the same evil means are employed in bad faith. And even good men in times of crises can be as ruthless as evil men—as Hochhuth's play *The Soldiers* so forcefully demonstrates. But the difference is that for those who have reached a plateau of self-consciousness about their condition, there is yet the possibility of transcendence; while for those who act in bad faith, the path to despair becomes one from which there is eventually No Exit.

Some may ask whether this study is not itself pornographic; for it does, after all, seek to represent despair as inescapable, to release (in the imagination) the demonic and irrational forces that have been repressed, and to force the reader to in fact experience himself at this level, in the hope that he will come to admit that this demonic element is a part of his real self. Do I not therefore run the risk of corrupting the imagination?

The answer is clearly "yes." But my pornography is therapeutic. The imagination of evil is the most effective way of exorcising ourselves of this evil; it is a source of self-transcendence. Its effect is cathartic. Mere pornography, because it has suspended the moral and critical framework, is self-perpetuating. Therapeutic pornography, precisely because it is both critical and imaginative, is transcendental. And transcendental pornography is prophetic; its purpose is not simply to describe and evoke evil but to supersede it.

3.

Let me now sum up what I think this book is all about. Traditionally, all speculations into human nature have been dominated by mythic structures having their origins in primordial experiences. At least four different structures have so far made themselves visible: the "mytho-poeic," the "teleological," the "empirical-rational," and the "absurd." In each case, the fundamental orientation is toward defining the limits of human responsibility and participation in the world process.

For the mytho-poeic outlook, responsibility is typically relegated to the arbitrary will of irrationally motivated spirits; under the teleological outlook, it lies in rational goals emanating from a pre-existing and rational source (whether it be nature or the gods); for the rational empirical mode, it lies both in the exercise of human reason in uncovering the laws of nature and in the subsequent application of that knowledge to the control of history; while from the standpoint of the absurd, responsibility is the exercise of creativity. What we now call the social sciences emerged under the teleological mode, first with the Greeks and later with the Christians. From approximately the period of the Renaissance, however, the teleological mode was seriously challenged by new ideas which viewed the fate of men as subject to the jurisdiction of Natural Law. This was the achievement of the combined effects of empiricism and rationalism. But the dialectic of history is such that once the structure of experience has been brought to conceptual clarity, the very nature of that experience is substantially altered. The net result of rational-empiricism is the "death of god" (which already begins with Hume), culminating in the experience of the absurd.

Our present world is very much dominated by the experience of the absurd, although we still pay homage to rationalistic models. We believe that history is driven by purposes, but experience does not support this belief. The result of the dissonance between expectation and experience is the phenomenon of apocalyptic nihilism. Instead of facing up to the absurd, we either counterfeit or ignore it. Many of our current myths and images of man (such as underlie the practice of the social sciences) have been surreptitiously manufactured for the purpose of counterfeiting the experience of the absurd. I propose to confront the absurd directly by imaginatively living through it. For a mind which has achieved an imaginative and critical awareness of the absurd is no longer subject to the limitations of absurdity, and may be said, therefore, to have transcended it.

This book may be regarded therefore as an exercise in the imagination of evil. It proceeds from the assumption that man's very being is ambivalent: he seeks both to be what he is not and not to be what he is; he is a being whose very being emerges through self-negation. From this concept we can better appreciate man's capacity for evil, and the ease with which the experience of power, a necessary consequence of our culture, facilitates this indulgence. For the most part this ambivalence has not yet been understood by Western man. Rational humanism has clouded the issue with its emphasis on reason, progress, and Utopia. Utopian thinking generates the myth that man's discomfort in the world is a result of institutions. Evil, it says, has its source in society. We ought, therefore, to use our power to correct society and to eliminate evil. Humanism has thus bred the present paranoia which is preoccupied with fighting evil, a preoccupation which rests on the bad faith of pretending that good is automatically realized through the elimination of evil.

The net result of humanism has therefore been what the psychiatrist R. D. Laing has called "mystification," a device through which truth is concealed by subterfuge; where, for example, violence is redefined as love. One experiences oneself at the primordial level as ambivalence. But humanism forces us to conform to the image of man which excludes the irrational. Hence the spontaneous expression of irrationality is regarded as "debased," and we have thereby been tricked out of our personal world of experience. We have been forced to murder the demonic in order to free the angelic. But we cannot escape the guilt induced by this self-betrayal, and the more angelic we become in practice the more self-alienated we become in spirit. Love itself and virtue become alienated responses.

But alienation is violence. Humanism breeds the socially conditioned hallucination, enforced by terror, that heaven and hell are separate places, and that one can find heaven by simply avoiding hell. The result is that life itself becomes a hell, the sort of place depicted, for example, in Edward Albee's plays, and most especially in *Who's Afraid of Virginia Woolf?* All of this is a result of our having "split being down the middle"—a naive separation of good and evil. This bifurcation of being is man's original sin and his eternal nemesis. As Laing puts it: "If we cling to the good without the bad, denying the one for the other, what happens is that the dissociated evil impulse, now evil in a double sense, returns to permeate and possess the good and turn it into itself." [3]

No wonder then that the history of Western man, in spite of its excessively rationalistic and humanistic traditions, has been so thoroughly permeated by violence. Laing again sums it up well when he writes:

In the last fifty years, we human beings have slaughtered by our own hands something like seventy million of our own species. We all live under constant threat of our total annihilation. We seem to seek death and destruction as much as life and happiness. We are driven, it seems, to kill and be killed as we are to live and let live. Only by the most outrageous violation of ourselves have we achieved our capacity to live in relative adjustment to civilization apparently driven to its own destruction. Perhaps to a limited extent we can undo what has been done to us, and what we have done to ourselves. Perhaps men and women were born to love one another, simply and genuinely, rather than to this travesty that we call love. If we can stop destroying ourselves we may stop destroying others. We have to begin by admitting and even accepting our violence, rather than blindly destroying ourselves with it, and therewith we have to realize that we are as deeply afraid to live and to love as we are to die.[4]

It is precisely with the purpose of admitting and somehow accepting our violence that this book is concerned. Against the background of the perennial conflict between humanistic and irrationalistic theories of man, I will introduce the myth of existential man, whose very being is to emerge through self-negation and whose salvation depends upon his ability to imaginatively live through, with the purpose of transcending, the implicit contradictions of his nature.

CHAPTER ONE. THE PROPAGANDA OF IRRATIONALISM AND THE CORRUPTION OF CULTURE

The process of specialization, departmentalization, and fragmentation, in the Humanities as well as in the Sciences, has reached a height undreamed of . . .
and we stand in greater need than ever of a Speculum mentis, a panoramic survey or chart of the intellectual world whereby some sense of The Whole as a whole may be attained and preserved.

Basil Willey

All thought is for the sake of action. We try to understand ourselves and our world only in order that we may learn how to live. The end of our self-knowledge is not the contemplation by enlightened intellects of their own mysterious nature, but the freer and more effectual self-revelation of that nature in a vigorous practical life.

R. G. Collingwood

The condition of freedom in any state is always a widespread and consistent skepticism of the canons upon which power insists.

Harold J. Laski

In 1939 John Dewey addressed a troubled generation with words that carry as much meaning today as they did then. Writing at a time when some men had begun to take freedom for granted, others were trying to achieve it, and some had already surrendered it, Dewey posed a number of probing questions which no generation fearful of its freedom and integrity can afford not to take seriously. Dewey wanted to know whether the desire for freedom is inherent in human nature or whether it is simply an acquired appetite which can just as easily be satisfied by less demanding goals; whether it is desired for its own sake or as a means of getting other things; and whether its possession entails such onerous responsibilities that the mass of men will readily surrender it for the sake of greater ease.

> Is the struggle for liberty so arduous that most men are easily distracted from the endeavor to achieve and maintain it? Does freedom in itself and in the things it brings with it seem as important as security of livelihood; as food, shelter, clothing, or even as having a good time? . . . Is love of liberty ever anything more than a desire to be liberated from some special restriction? And when it is got rid of does the desire for liberty die down until something else feels intolerable? Again, how does the desire for freedom compare in intensity with the desire to feel equal with others, especially with those who have previously been called superiors? How do the fruits of liberty compare with the enjoyments that spring from a feeling of union, of solidarity, with others? Will men surrender their liberties if they believe that in doing so they will obtain the satisfaction that comes from a sense of fusion with others and that respect by others which is the product of strength furnished by solidarity? [1]

No serious attempt to answer such questions can avoid raising other questions about the scientific and metaphysical status of human nature. Is there such a thing as human nature at all? What can we say about it? Can there be a genuine science of human nature, or will any attempt to construct such a science suffer from the limitations that according to James Harvey Robinson are indigenous to the very concept of a science of man?

> We like to continue to believe what we have been accustomed to accept as true, and the resentment aroused when doubt is cast upon any of our assumptions leads us to seek every manner of excuse for clinging to them. *The result is that most of our so-called reasoning consists in finding arguments for going on believing as we already do.* . . . And now the astonishing and perturbing suspicion emerges that perhaps almost all that has passed for social science, political economy, politics, and ethics in the past may be brushed aside by future generations as mainly rationalizing.[2]

Notwithstanding the force and seriousness of Robinson's remarks, the reflections that make up the content of this book are premised on the convictions, first, that an objective and truthful answer to the question, Who is Man?, is possible, and second, that such an achievement is indeed a *conditio sine qua non* of the very survival of man as man. The dignity and freedom of man are functions of his self-knowledge. Hence, rather than become alarmed by the apparent skepticism of Robinson's remark, I prefer to draw attention to its implicit truth: that any attempt to answer the question, Who is Man?, takes its shape from an answer to the more subjectively centered question, Who am I? The study of man, in other words, proceeds from an existential-phenomenological interpretation of experience, one which seeks to explain the human condition from the standpoint of the agent rather than the observer. This interpretation seeks to ground the structure of social reality in the agent's experience of being-in-the-world. The social world thus becomes the product of the agent's motives, intentions, and choices, a place in which individuals emerge as persons by pursuing goals of their own choosing in the presence of others with whom they are inter-subjectively related.

I would argue, for this reason, against those who would deny that the gap between subjectivity and objectivity can ever in fact be bridged. Subjectivity is not a threat to objectivity but is, on the contrary, the very condition of its possibility. The Who am I? question (which explores the agent's lived-experience of the world) is the most crucial of all questions about man, not simply because it offers a framework for comprehending the objective structure of the social world, but also because the asking of the question is itself important in shaping a person's humanity. This is what Socrates meant when he said that the unexamined life was not worth living. He was declaring that the Who am I? question had priority over all other questions.

Various reasons can be given to support the claim that an adequate understanding of human nature—in the form of what some philosophers would call a "philosophical anthropology"—is a necessary condition not only of the social studies, but also of one's very attempt to be human. But the most important reason is the now accepted conviction that the image man has of himself, his answer to the question, Who am I?, is one of the most powerful variables affecting his behavior. And if we know anything for certain in social science, it is that the image a man has of himself is not innate but acquired; it is acquired in much the same way that a person acquires a habit or a personality trait. We know also that so far as the relation between self-image and behavior is concerned, the operant factor is not whether that image is *true* but whether it is *believed*. If a man accepts a certain image of himself, he will often behave according to it, then mistakenly accept this behavior as evidence of the truth of his self-image.[3] It is, in other words, entirely possible that one's image of oneself, whether or not it is well founded i.e., has a basis in reality), may become a "self-fulfilling prophecy." As Thomas Pettigrew puts it:

> If . . . you believe the world to be a hostile place, you will probably act in such a manner as to cause the world to become in fact hostile towards you. In this sense a person's own beliefs about a social situation can contribute to shaping the situation. Such beliefs, then, are "self-fulfilling prophecies." [4]

There are two kinds of "self-fulfilling prophecies." Some provide the dynamics for a creative and healthy self-making process, while others give rise to self-contradictory and self-destructive processes of self-making. In the history of Western culture, man's image of himself has been significantly shaped by the contest between various types of mythologies, such as the myth of "rational man" (according to which society is a vehicle for the virtuous expression of man's innate capacity for reasonableness and humane conduct) and the myth of "irrational man" (according to which society is a vehicle for the expression, repression, and control of man's innate capacity for aggressiveness). Other myths which have arisen are the myth of man as a *tabula rasa*, whose nature and character are entirely products of the environment, and the myth of existential man, who begins as a "nothingness" and creates a character for himself through choice. Finally, there are myths which mediate between extremes, combining elements of each into new patterns. As a result, the present age is prolific with myths.

Myths are also covert value judgments which determine the limits of human responsibility. To view the world from a particular mythology is to assume a characteristic moral outlook. Consider, for example, the image which depicts man as a mere effect of environmental manipulation. Many would like to pretend that this image is justified by the evidence at hand. But, more likely, the very selection of evidence, indeed the entire causal analysis, is itself determined by the image. The argument that the social sciences are value-free *because* they are scientific falls to the possibility that they have become scientific *in order to be* value-free. Suspicion mounts that the driving force of scientism is now fed by the unconscious need to escape from the responsibility of taking a moral stand and of evaluating the human condition from a moral point of view. We have not, in other words, come to deprive man of responsibility for his own conduct because the evidence requires us to; rather, we have first chosen to embrace this image so that we may discover the evidence and turn consciousness into a mere object. Such an attitude may be reasonable with respect to physical nature, but for human nature it is thoroughly irrational.

The traditional sciences of man, through consciousness of their inherent presuppositions, subject their values to critical appraisal. The contemporary sciences, through the bad faith of pretending to be value-free, allow values to creep in unnoticed and to permeate and influence society uncriticized. This is the real difference between the two sciences. And there is nothing more dangerous to the health of a society than to be influenced by uncritically accepted values—which is precisely what follows from the dogma that the social sciences are value-free.

2. THE PATHOLOGY OF THE SOCIAL AND HUMAN STUDIES

Within the social studies (gratuitously referred to by many of its practitioners as the social sciences) there is a growing discrepancy between thought and action (or research and ethical commitment) as currently manifested in the widespread belief that a scientist has no interest in the ethical implications of his research. This corruption has its roots in the mythology that regards man as a *tabula rasa* whose behavior and character are entirely products of the environment. If the individual is not responsible for his character, then how can the scientist (who is, after all, just a special kind of individual) be responsible for the results of his research (which is, of course, just a special kind of behavior)?

A classic statement of the ideology that underlies the social scientist's concept of limited social responsibility is the following remark by Abraham Flexner:

> To be sure, the social scientist must find his material in the thick of events; but qua scientist he must select and approach and frame his problems, from the viewpoint of science, without incurring the responsibility for policies. In the social as in the physical sciences, the university is, insofar as scientific effort to understand phenomena is concerned, indifferent to the effect and use of truth . . . it is one thing to incur responsibility for policies, and quite another to set up an experiment primarily in the interest of ascertaining truth or testing theory. The modern university must neither fear nor make itself responsible for its conduct.[5]

The spirit of this remark is well illustrated by the style with which many social scientists set out to investigate the causes of social evils. A typical case is the sociology of race prejudice. Thus, for example, finding out that Negroes are harshly discriminated against, and describing the conditions under which such discrimination arises, is all too often kept thoroughly separate from any question about the morality of race prejudice. Under the protective cover of this ideology, some social scientists have even discovered that once you have explained the *causes* of a phenomenon you have somehow *justified* it as well; there is no longer any need to take a moral stand for or against it. I regard this ideology as an expression of what R. G. Collingwood called "The Propaganda of Irrationalism," [6] the attempt to provide a rational basis for the irrational flight from responsibility. When allowed to infect the tissues of the social sciences it becomes a device through which the world of values is magically transformed into an ethically neutral system of dependent, independent, and intervening variables: as in the currently fashionable tendency to reduce all ethical behavior, whether of individuals or groups, to variables of a purely psychological and sociological nature. This not only eliminates the need to take a moral stand, it makes moral indifference scientifically respectable. I am thinking particularly of recent efforts to interpret such phenomena as Negro sit-ins, civil rights demonstrations, and, indeed, any public action directed toward social goals as cases of "pro-social acting out of unconscious aggression" caused by "deprivation of parental affection," or as "ways of resolving problems of identity and superego formation," and so on.

The following example is taken from an important and influential paper by Drs. Jacob R. Fishman and Frederic Solomon, which deals with the phenomenon of "Youth and Social Action" in general and with Negro sit-ins in particular.[7] Following the well-trodden path established by Erik Erikson, the authors argue to the conclusion that such behavior is usually motivated by an "identity crisis." The Negro youth's social protest, in the name of justice, against the injustices of white society, forms a pattern of identity growth. Through the force of the various moral and democratic principles they invoke to justify their action, Negro demonstrators are able to channel aggression into a positive identification with the traditional ego-ideals of the white majority as well as with that of the world community,[8] all of which provides a basis for the development of their own personalities. Pro-social acting out is therefore an expression of unconscious needs, a way of acting out early childhood frustrations, deprivations, and parental conflicts and wishes. When the individual claims to see his behavior in terms of conscience and morality, he is really testifying to the strength of his superego, which, having become incorporated into his self-image, now functions as a source of motivation.

In short, according to Drs. Fishman and Solomon, acting out in the name of the ideology of justice has an important role in identity formation and progressive development of ego functions.[9]

> . . . one can find in the student sit-in movement patterns of
> adolescent identity-striving similar to those in many other
> adolescent groups. Through the influence of the current value
> system are filtered the typical internal pressures and new ego
> capacities of early and late adolescence. Public action for
> social goals is their way of at least temporarily resolving issues
> of identity formation, conscience, and aggression.[10]

But in such accounts, as Paul Goodman once complained,
"There is no mention of simple justice, of human indignation
at being insulted, or of the ingenuous political effort of youth
to make a safer and happier world." [11] Goodman cites examples like the above as evidence of the "political pathology of
present social science method." I am tempted to go even
further and argue that when matters of justice and morality
are so handled, the practice of social science becomes implicitly "pornographic." It is at least implicitly pornographic
because (notwithstanding the sincere and legitimate intentions of the investigators), in the absence of any other purpose, the inquiry draws its strength not from its disinterested
scientific or explanatory value but from its character as "exposé"; that is to say, from its "entertainment value." And it
is pornographic also because it encourages those who are
driven by neurotic impulses to exploit the world of social
action for their own narcissistic purposes, thus turning the
theory into a self-fulfilling prophecy.

But worse still, just as it is possible to reduce virtue to
variables having to do with an individual's pathology, so
it is equally possible to denude the phenomenon of evil by
reducing it to the level of a mere spectacle. Under the influence of the disinterested science of behavior, evil ceases to be
regarded as an "outrage" to be experienced in anguish. It
becomes instead an expression of "banality" or a form of
"pathology"—or, better still, a "deviation from accepted
norms," to be understood for what it is and then explained.
Such responses to evil are symptoms of what Karl Mannheim
has called "a crisis in valuation." [12] The crisis in valuation is

the loss of the capacity to evaluate phenomena according to genuinely ethical considerations.

I have no complaint with the effort to construct a causal analysis of human behavior. What I am really complaining about is the tendency to reduce the *evaluation* of the "intentionality" and "moral significance" of human behavior to the *causal explanation* of that behavior. Among the greatest of all evils is the compulsion to reduce the concrete to the abstract—precisely what this reduction of quality to quantity virtually amounts to. The consequences of this reduction will become clear once we understand what is entailed by the *evaluation* of human actions. To evaluate and appreciate the morality of an action is to incur certain responsibilities with respect to one's own ethical commitments. In judging another's actions as morally sound, I commit myself to acting in a manner which is commensurate with my judgment. Likewise, to judge another's actions as evil is to commit myself to taking a moral stand against them. But to denude that behavior altogether of its moral qualities by reducing these qualities to the underlying causes of that behavior is a convenient way of escaping from the anguish of taking a moral stand. It is one thing to identify the causes of behavior knowing that although they are logically independent of the intentionality and moral significance of the behavior, they will nevertheless become a part of human consciousness once they are revealed (i.e., in the sense that they may radically alter the essence of the human condition, hence giving rise to new possibilities of moral behavior). But it is quite another matter to depersonalize that behavior by applying the results of one's causal analysis to eliminate systematically the moral issues involved, while all the time pretending this will have no moral effect on the subject of investigation. The former is a legitimate scientific enterprise; the latter is a counterfeit, which draws its strength from the widespread acceptance of an ideology that virtually repudiates the rapprochement between theory and practice by creating a false and abstract separation between fact and value, and then pleading indifference to the possible moral effects which our inquiries into human behavior may have on man's future behavior.

It is of course essential that science is never allowed to erode in the service of an ideology. The scientist must never become a mere apologist for the establishment, a mere hewer of wood and drawer of water for those who seek to control political power. But neither must he be permitted the excuse of pleading ethical neutrality. In particular, when it comes to the diagnosis of human action and social change the scientist must accept the inevitability that his work is itself a variable in shaping the phenomenon he is studying. We may begin with the credo that while life itself is of course charged with values (such as, for example, the beliefs in individuality, responsibility, freedom, morality, choice, and so on), science is value free. But the result of this credo is that we are soon told that life itself must become more scientific. And since science has been allowed to define itself as the essentially value-free act *par excellence*, so life will become more scientific only as it becomes less charged with values. Thus does the "dehumanizing" of science conceived as a specialized activity within a culture lead inevitably to the dehumanization of culture itself. In short, social science is a form of social action, and for this reason is potentially an instrument of great power: in which case it must be regarded as subject to the same mechanisms that underlie the dynamics of any other form of power.[13]

If the social scientist is to fulfill his social and moral responsibilities, he must, as it were, join forces with the poet: so that in addition to describing and explaining the conditions of despair, he can also communicate what it means to feel defeated and despised, to belong emotionally to the ranks of the dispossessed. For without this existential "identification of consciousness," the results of social science can never provide a responsible basis for moral evaluation. And if social inquiry cannot achieve a genuine "understanding" of the "felt interiority" of the phenomenon in question, it can never properly become a factor in "choosing" how to act. So long as the drama of man's search for humanity continues to be represented through abstractions alone—as, for example, when the revolt against injustice is represented as essentially a way of resolving unconscious conflicts—no real concern and respect for the basic humanity of man's behavior and the ethical goals toward which such behavior is directed can be expected either from the actors or the audience. Or, as E. E. Cummings once put it:

> beware of heartless them,
> [given a scalpel, they dissect a kiss;
> or, sold the reason, they undream a dream.] [14]

Ralph Ellison has recently brought similar charges against academic sociology's way of dealing with Negro life in America. His complaint is that it reduces the dignity of that life to theoretical clichés.[15] Take, for example, the typical representation of the Negro family as broken, matriarchal, dominated by a male-castrating mother, and so on. Ellison protests that to accept this image of the Negro as a statement of reality is to destroy the dignity of Negro life. If you think this way then you can never learn to use your own eyes and your own heart. And for the writer to accept it means the death of his art.

I don't deny that these sociological formulas are drawn from life, but I do deny that they define the complexity of Harlem. They only abstract it and reduce it to proportions which the sociologists can manage. I simple don't recognize Harlem in them. And I certainly don't recognize the people of Harlem whom I know. Which is by no means to deny the ruggedness of life there, nor the hardship, the poverty, the sordidness, the filth. But there is something else in Harlem, something subjective, willful, and complexly and compellingly human. It is "that something else" that challenges the sociologists who ignore it, and the society which would deny its existence. It is that "something else" which makes for our strength, which makes for our endurance and our promise. This is the proper subject for the Negro American writer. Hell, he doesn't have to spend all the tedious time required to write novels simply to repeat what the sociologists and certain white intellectuals are broadcasting like a zoo full of parrots—*and* getting much more money for it than most Negro writers will ever see. If he does this he'll not only go on begging, but worse, he'll lie to his people, discourage their interest in literature, and emasculate his own talent.[16]

But the most serious indictment of all is Ellison's charge that academic sociologists have become demagogues and pornographers of despair. The sociology of Negro life in America is today a most lucrative enterprise. By specializing in the exposé of Negro poverty and despair, the sociologist adds to his own "wealth" and further enslaves the subjects upon whose suffering he profits, thus ensuring a perpetuation of the evils into which he will continue to inquire.

. . . today the sociologists are up to their necks in politics and have access to millions of governmental dollars, which, I'm afraid, have been secured at the cost of propagating an image of the Negro condition which is apt to destroy our human conception of ourselves just at the moment when we are becoming politically free.[17]

What Ellison and others like myself are now concerned about was long ago expressed by James Agee. Agee was one of the first to alert us to the dangers inherent in the sociology of despair when in 1940 he first published his remarkable study of the life-world of a family of tenant farmers in Alabama. The study was originally commissioned by the federal government, which wanted a well-researched piece of academic sociology. But as Agee reflected on what he was doing, he began to suffer a strange conversion: he gradually realized that he had taken a human world and turned it into a laboratory, and that beneath the façade he had erected in the name of science was a real human situation in which the researcher had assumed the godlike privilege of passing judgment on others. As a result, Agee produced, instead of a research report, a prose poem he called *Let Us Now Praise Famous Men*. His own description of the rationale underlying his conversion, as stated in the introduction to his book, is a classic indictment of what I have previously referred to as the pornography of despair masquerading as a science:

> It seems to me curious, not to say obscene and thoroughly terrifying, that it could occur to an association of human beings drawn together through need and chance and for profit into a company, an organ of journalism, to pry intimately into the lives of an undefended and appallingly damaged group of human beings, an ignorant and helpless rural family, for the purpose of parading the nakedness, disadvantage, and humiliation of these lives before another group of human beings, in the name of science of "honest journalism" (whatever that paradox may mean), of humanity, of social fearlessness, for money, and for a reputation for crusading and for unbias which, when skillfully enough qualified, is exchangeable at any bank for money (and in politics, for votes, job patronage, abelincolnism, etc.) . . . All of this, I repeat, seems to me curious, obscene, terrifying, and unfathomably mysterious.[18]

In contrast to the commonly employed techniques of academic sociology, Agee chose instead a radically different approach, best described in his own words.

> For in the immediate world, everything is to be discerned, for him who can discern it, and centrally and simply, without either dissection into science, or digestion into art, but with the whole of consciousness, seeking to perceive it as it stands; so that the aspect of a street in sunlight can roar in the heart of itself as a symphony, perhaps as no symphony can: and all of consciousness is shifted from the imagined, the revisive, to the effort to perceive simply the cruel radiance of what is.
>
> This is why the camera seems to me, next to unassisted and weaponless consciousness, the central instrument of our time; and is why in turn I feel such rage at its misuse: which has

spread so nearly universal a corruption of sight that I know of less than a dozen alive whose eyes I can trust even so much as my own.

If I had explained myself clearly you would realize by now that through this non-"artistic" view, this effort to suspend or destroy imagination, there opens before consciousness, and within it, a universe luminous, spacious, incalculably rich and wonderful in each detail, as related and natural to the human swimmer, and as full of glory, as his breathing; and that it is possible to capture and communicate this universe not so well by any means of art as through such open terms as I am trying it under.[19]

The ultimate aim of Agee's non-academic approach is not to classify and explain but to understand what it "feels" like to exist humanly. As in the case of Ralph Ellison, Agee too does not want to lose sight of the "dignity" of man, even when suffering the most impoverished of existences. What Agee aims to reveal about the people he writes about is not their depravity alone but rather the great weight, mystery, and nobility of their existence.

. . . these I will write of are human beings, living in this world, innocent of such twistings as . . . are taking place over their heads; [namely] that they were dwelt among, investigated, spied on, revered, and loved, by other quite monstrously alien human beings . . . who have picked up their living as casually as if it were a book, and who were actuated towards this reading by various possible reflexes of sympathy, curiosity, idleness, et cetera, and almost certainly in a lack of consciousness, and conscience, remotely appropriate to the enormity of what they are doing.[20]

It is the purpose of my book to unveil further the mystery of human existence and to investigate the possible origins of that peculiar behavior that leads not only to the pornographic exploitation of human misery and despair but also to the pornographic pursuit of power (one of the chief sources of that misery and despair). I am writing for all those who have a soft place in their hearts for speculations into the ambivalence of the human condition; for those whose reverence for the pursuit of self-knowledge is such that not only would they gladly risk falling into error and out of grace for the sake of it, but they would even risk trading the security of "certainty" and "objectivity" (ideology, dogma, and such) for a more honest but thoroughly self-critical understanding.

3. THE CORRUPTION OF HUMAN NATURE

Among the most dramatic examples of corruption within human nature itself is the recent acceleration of extremism in American political life and social behavior which has given rise to what Richard Hofstadter has called "the paranoid style of living and thinking." [21] Just as the pathology of social science derives from a separation of thought and action, which takes the form of pleading indifference to the ethical implications of research, so one of the chief sources of cultural paranoia is the ever-widening rift between the beliefs of a people and their actual behavior, and the tacit assumption among these same people that this duplicity, this contradiction between idealism and practice, is a normal state of affairs. In such a society, hypocrisy and moral turpitude become what Erich Fromm calls "socially patterned defects." [22] A socially patterned defect arises when the members of a society confuse "consensual validation" with "rational justification." That is to say, individuals naively assume that because a majority of people share certain ideals and feelings, these ideals and feelings are valid and true. Consensual validation thus provides a mechanism which permits the majority within a society to live with a defect without feeling guilty or neurotic about it. Acting contrary to our ideals, traditions, and beliefs can become such a defect. The individual shares it with many others and is therefore not aware of it as a defect. Hypocrisy is accepted as a normal property of life, and hypocritical behavior does not, therefore, arouse an experience of being different; of being, by virtue of one's hypocrisy, an outcast from society. What the hypocrite may have lost in integrity and a genuine feeling of happiness is made up for by the security of fitting in with the rest of mankind as he knows them.

No better example of the consequences of the failure of a people to live up to their basic presuppositions can be cited than the deterioration of Greek culture during the late fifth and early fourth centuries B.C., during the latter stages of the Peloponnesian Wars. In the early part of the fifth century B.C., the Athenian culture had risen to incredible heights of sophistication. But by the middle of the fourth century the "glory that was Greece" was slowly crumbling into a world of cynicism, despair, and corruption. Among the reasons which many historians have offered for the decline of the Greek world, great importance is placed on the various wars which resulted in the Greeks being conquered first by the Macedonians and then by the Romans. In much the same way, the decline of Rome is blamed on the barbarian invasions. But the Greek and Roman cultures were not destroyed by wars and barbarian invasions. What destroyed these cultures was their failure to keep alive in their actual conduct the fundamental presuppositions and ideals upon which they were built.

Notice, for example, how readily the Athenian demagogues place the responsibility for the breakup of Greek society on Spartan conspiracies, and on treasonous acts by persons like Socrates and Euripides, rather than on the failure of the Athenian people as a whole (and especially their military and political leaders) to live up to the basic beliefs upon which the Athenian democracy was founded. The most dramatic example of this failure is the almost unbelievable contrast between the ideals of democracy as expressed in Pericles' famous funeral oration delivered in the year 430 B.C., at the end of the first year of the war between Athens and Sparta, and the actual behavior of the Athenian army, some seventeen years later, toward the end of the war. In the year 430 Pericles addressed the Athenian nation with words that still stand as an inspiration for all who believe in the democratic view of human society:

> Our constitution is called a democracy because power is in the hands not of a minority but of the whole people. When it is a question of settling private disputes, everyone is equal before the law; when it is a question of putting one person before another in positions of public responsibility, what counts is not membership in a particular class but the actual ability which the man possesses. No one, so long as it is in him to be of service to the state, is kept in political obscurity because of poverty. And just as our political life is free and open, so is our day-to-day life in our relations to each other. We do not get into a quarrel with our next-door neighbor if he enjoys himself in his own way, nor do we give him the kind of black looks which, though they do no real harm, still do hurt people's feelings. We are free and tolerant in our private lives; but in public affairs we keep to the laws. This is because it commands our deep respect. We give our obedience to those whom we put in positions of authority, and we obey the laws themselves, especially those which are for the protection of the oppressed, and those unwritten laws which it is an acknowledged shame to break.
>
> Again, in questions of general good feeling there is a great contrast between us and most people. We make friends by doing good to others, not by receiving good from them. This makes our friendship all the more reliable, since we want to keep alive the gratitude of those who are in our debt by showing continued good will to them: whereas the feelings of one who owes us something lack the same enthusiasm, since he knows that, when he repays our kindness, it will be more like paying back a debt than giving something spontaneously. . . . Taking everything together, then, I declare that our city is an education to Greece, and I declare that in my opinion each single one of our citizens, in all the manifold aspects of life, is

able to show himself the rightful lord and owner of his own person, and do this, moreover, with exceptional grace and exceptional versatility. . . . Athens alone of the states we know, comes to her testing time in a greatness that surpasses what was imagined of her. In her case, and in her case alone, no invading enemy is ashamed at being defeated, and no subject can complain of being governed by people unfit for their responsibilities. Mighty indeed are the marks and monuments of our empire which we have left. Future ages will wonder at us, as the present age wonders at us now. . . . Our adventurous spirit has forced an entry into every sea and into every land; and everywhere we have left behind us everlasting memorials of good done to our friends or suffering inflicted on our enemies.[23]

Future ages have indeed wondered at the everlasting memorials of good done to the friends of Athens and the suffering inflicted on her enemies—such as, for example, the invasion by the Athenian army of the island of Melos in the year 416.[24] No enemy, said Pericles, need be ashamed of being conquered by Athens. But in the year 416 it was the Athenians themselves who were ashamed, not by the humiliation of having been conquered but by the brutality of their own conquests. Pericles had expressed the ideal of Greek democracy. Within two decades the Athenian generals demonstrated how easily and how quickly ideals can be corrupted. On this occasion, as reported by Thucydides, the Athenians attempted to persuade the Melians to violate their oath of neutrality in order to enter, with Athens, into a coalition against the combined forces of Sparta. The Melians, however, preferred their neutrality and their freedom and even appealed to the Periclean principles of democracy: the principles of justice, self-determination, and fair play, which they naively believed to govern Athenian foreign policy. At this point the Athenian generals lost patience and declared that they no longer intended to use such fine phrases as "freedom, honor, and justice," concerning what is right and what is wrong. They recommended instead that both sides speak their real thoughts; for surely the Melians knew as well as they that "when these matters are discussed by practical people, the standard of justice depends upon the equality of power to compel, and that in fact the strong do what they have the power to do and the weak accept what they have to accept." The difference between right and wrong is simply the difference between strength and weakness. The quarrel between Athens and Melos is no fair fight with honor on one side and shame on the other. It is rather a question of saving one's life and not resisting those who are too strong. "Do not," said the Athenians, "be like those people who miss the chance of saving themselves by turning in their adversity, when every hope has left them, to what is vague and blind, to prophecies and oracles and such things as by encouraging false hope lead men to ruin." The generals went on to explain that their behavior in this instance was justified by being in accordance with the laws of nature. "Our knowledge of men," they declared, "leads us to conclude that it is a general and necessary law of nature to rule where one can. This is not a law that we made ourselves, nor were we the first to act upon it when it was made. We found it already in existence, and we shall leave it to exist forever among those who come after us. We are merely acting in accordance with it, and we know that you or anyone else with the same power as ours would be acting in precisely the same way." Thus is the behavior of power politics conceived as an expression of natural law. 1462429

The Melians were, of course, defeated by the Athenians, who immediately put to death all men of military age whom they took, and sold the women and children as slaves. Many Athenians were shocked by the brutality of their army. Few realized, however, that the behavior of the army was an expression of the whole character of Athenian society and not just a result of the arbitrary will of a few generals. If the behavior of the army was corrupt, it was because the very soul of Athens, whose spirit was represented by the army, was itself corrupt.

For us, the deterioration of Greek culture contains a message of profound and ominous significance. A critical examination of our own society shows that we too have begun to behave contrary to our beliefs. And we too have come to accept this duplicity as a natural fact, thus transforming our hypocrisy into a standard for our young to live up to. The real threat to our survival is not the existence of foreign totalitarian states but the failure within our society to meet the demands of our own cultural goals. The real enemy is the loss of faith in our principles and beliefs. It is a sign of genuine sickness when an entire nation permits itself the indulgence of pretending that it may openly violate all of the sacred principles from which it was originally born and still survive. But it is characteristic of the paranoid mentality never to assume responsibility for its personal failures. Hence the almost neurotic obsession within paranoid societies to place the blame on such things as outside pressures, organized conspiracies by alien governments, and so on. Where else but in a paranoid society will you find such an institution as an "Un-American Activities Committee" whose chief function consists in investigating (so that it can discredit) the very expressions of freedom—namely, dissent and open criticism of government policies—which according to most historians gave rise to the American nation in the first place.[25]

As a further example of what happens when a society fails to live up to its implicit beliefs, I cite an incident which occurred in 1961 and which raises some important questions about the morality of the American bombing of Hiroshima at the close of the Second World War. The incident has to do with the strange behavior of Major Claude Eatherly, who claimed to have been responsible for the Hiroshima mission and who as a result of his strange and unorthodox public confession of guilt (involving an attempt on his part to awaken a sense of responsibility within the entire nation) was "officially" declared insane at a full-fledged public "lunacy" hearing in Waco, Texas, in January 1961, and thereby "removed" from society.

Admittedly there has been some controversy about the accuracy and reliability of Eatherly's story, and about the integrity of the legend that has grown up around him. At least one writer, William Bradford Huie, with the warm support of many of his reviewers, has virtually accused Eatherly of being a publicity-seeking fraud who grossly exaggerated his role in the Hiroshima incident. According to Huie, there is little question that Eatherly was insane, and in his book *The Hiroshima Pilot* Huie supports the court's decision to incarcerate Eatherly in a mental hospital. So far as the *legend* is concerned, it is, according to Huie, the result of distortions which are at variance with available records. On the question of Eatherly's alleged feelings of guilt, it is Huie's opinion that this judgment is not only questionable (i.e., has been supported by only a minority of psychiatrists while being rejected by a much larger number) but also quite improbable.[26] Huie therefore argues, throughout his book, that Eatherly suffered more from neglect than from guilt; that he cunningly invented his guilt in order to dramatize and publicize himself; that he deliberately committed bizarre crimes, not to court punishment for his sense of guilt but to appeal to the compassion of the court and hence avoid imprisonment, and, finally, to increase his disability pension— which is considerably larger for those who can prove to have suffered serious psychological damage as a result of the war.

But Huie has in turn been criticized by Ronnie Dugger, who in *Dark Star* (1967) attempts to restore the integrity of the Eatherly legend. Dugger's point, which seems to me incontestable, is that whether Eatherly was really the navigator in charge or merely one small link in the chain of events which led to the bombing, and whether he was or was not totally sane, the moral and symbolic significance of the story still stands: a significance whose essence is most eloquently summed up by Bertrand Russell, in his preface to the English edition of Eatherly's letters.

The case of Claude Eatherly is not only one of appalling and prolonged injustice to an individual, but is also symbolic of the suicidal madness of our time. No unbiased person, after reading Eatherly's letters, can honestly doubt his sanity, and I find it very difficult to believe that the doctors who pronounced him insane were persuaded of the accuracy of their own testimony. He has been punished solely because he repented of his comparatively innocent participation in a wanton act of mass murder. The steps that he took to awaken men's consciences to our present insanity were, perhaps, not always the wisest that could have been taken, but they were actuated by motives which deserve the admiration of all who are capable of feelings of humanity. The world was prepared to honor him for his part in the massacre, but, when he repented, it turned against him, seeing in his act of repentance its own condemnation.[27]

In short, the significance of the incident has to do first of all with the fact that when an individual rose to question the morality of an official act, the effect of his criticism was neutralized by branding him insane; in much the same way, for example, that both agitators for civil rights and critics of American war policy in Vietnam are continuously discredited by branding their behavior pathological, cowardly, treasonous, and so on.[28] And, in the second place, the Eatherly incident very clearly reveals the importance, for the preservation of the moral outlook, of acknowledging that there are some occasions on which the individual must be prepared to assume responsibility for the unintended as well as the intended consequences of his acts. To plead the excuse that the consequences were unintended (and therefore I am not responsible for them), or even that the act itself was no more than the fulfillment of a command, is virtually to opt out of the requirements of morality.

The issues involved in the Eatherly case were first brought to public attention by the German philosopher Gunther Anders. In an open letter to President Kennedy, dated January 13, 1961, Anders protested the official decision to declare Eatherly insane.[29] The basis of the decision had been Eatherly's feeling of guilt concerning an act for which he in fact bore no real responsibility and which eventually led to his pathological behavior of deliberately breaking the law. In other words, Eatherly was judged insane because of his abnormal reactions to the Hiroshima incident. But, Anders declares, in a passage of profound importance:

> Every reasonable medical man knows that it is abnormal to act normally during or after an abnormal situation; it is abnormal if, after an appalling shock, someone goes on living as if nothing had happened. This is true all the more so, if the shock transcends all proportion and all "holding capacity" which a human being can visualize, digest, remember, or repent—and such is the case in question. For Eatherly left behind him the ashes of hundreds of thousands of people and of a city which one second before had been vibrant with life. If he reacted "abnormally," he reacted adequately. For cases of inadequately weak reactions, academic psychology has even introduced a special term, "seelenblindheit" (soul blindness). A classical illustration of such "soul blindness" is, for instance, the well-known though ill-reputed reply of your predecessor Truman who, asked on the occasion of his 75th birthday whether any incident in his long life had caused him any pain or regret, answered: yes, he deeply regretted not to have married earlier. Hiroshima didn't come to his mind. Or, in the words of Lessing: "He who doesn't lose his mind over certain things, has none to lose."

Moreover, to isolate "criminal actions" (as those strange hold-ups of Eatherly) instead of understanding them as reactions, is unscientific and not worthy of the medical profession. It is as if, witnessing a man clubbed to death, we would confine ourselves to registering the unusual loudness of his screaming and, ignoring the enormity of what is being done to him, would consider his shrieks as a symptom of his abnormality. Unfortunately, there is a strong probability that the doctors have isolated Eatherly's reactions in just this way, that they skimmed them off from the actions to which they were reactions. For the doctors have spoken of a "guilt complex," thereby trying to talk those familiar only with the fashion words of science into believing that the guilt feeling in question was unjustified, unreasonable, and thus classifiable only as "pathological." In painful vulgarization of a psycho-analytical school term, they even dared to speak in his case of an "Oedipus Complex"—as though an incest desire lay at the root of his behavior and not the never-to-be-forgotten picture of thousands of corpses. May I observe, *en marge,* that such silly and undignified exploitation of scientific vocabulary—committed in order to ornament half-truths with the dignity of science—has for years now undermined the reputation of the United States, at least in the eyes of educated circles, all over the world.[30]

As represented by his letters to Gunther Anders, Eatherly was tormented by the anguish of, on the one hand, seeking insight into the enormity of an event which had occurred with horrifying mechanical smoothness, while at the same time trying to understand how it was possible for him and others like him to be celebrated as national heroes. His behavior, then, far from being abnormal, was, from a moral standpoint, a thoroughly normal reaction to the painful discrepancy he sensed between his guilt and the glamour forced upon him. Since his participation in the Hiroshima mission was not recognized as a crime, he would have to devise other methods in order to enforce the penalty to which he felt entitled, which is precisely what he did. Through his sham criminal actions, Eatherly tried to enforce that punishment which was not granted him, and, to cite his own words, "to shatter the 'hero image' of me by which society has sought to perpetuate its own complacency." [31]

But his act was also prophetic. And, as is the fate of prophets, Eatherly was devoured by his society. As Eatherly himself put it in a letter to Anders: "The truth is that society cannot accept the fact of my guilt without at the same time recognizing its own far deeper guilt." [32] Upon reading this sentence, writes Anders, "one can only conclude: happy the times in which the insane speak out this way, wretched the times in which only the insane speak out this way." [33]

The most serious aspect of the Eatherly incident is the question of collective responsibility. Eatherly's critics magically absolve him of responsibility by appealing to the principle of "co-acting." He was, after all, only following orders: which is precisely the principle to which Eichmann and other Nazis appealed in their defense against the charge of having committed crimes against humanity, a defense which was unequivocally repudiated at Nuremberg.

But Eatherly is anything but the twin of Eichmann. He is, as Anders has put it:

> . . . his great and hope-inspiring opposite—not the man who passes off machinery as a pretext for renouncing conscience, but, on the contrary, the man who recognizes machinery as the fatal danger to conscience. Here he strikes at the very core of the moral problem of today. For if we point to the apparatus into which we are incorporated as nothing but ignorant "cogs," and if we accept the alleged excuse, "We were not acting but merely co-acting," as being justified under all circumstances, then we abolish the freedom of moral decision and the freedom of conscience. Then we even degrade the word "free," and make the expression "free world" into an empty and hypocritical protestation. I am afraid we are already very close to this.
>
> The greatness of Eatherley's behavior consists precisely in the courage with which he turns this argument upside down. With his behavior he tries to demonstrate that, morally speaking, there is no such thing as mere "co-acting." Whatever we are doing, promoting or provoking by merely "co-acting," is being done by us. We have to answer not only for our own individual acts, but also for the team acts in which we just participate or are made to participate. The question of our conscience is not only, "How should we act?" but also "Where and how far may we or may we not, ought we or ought we not 'co-act'?" Eatherly feels even more responsible for his participation than for his individual and private acts, since the effects of private acts, compared with the catastrophic consequences of the acts in which we only participate, have become utterly insignificant. To be blameless in private life is child's play; custom replaces conscience to a great extent. It is, on the contrary, before the sweet terror of the powers that make us conform and co-function where real independence

and real civil courage are required. If this attitude (and this is Eatherly's position with regard to the atomic stockpiling policy of your country) consists of courageous refusal, then the devil's circle of mere co-acting is perforated, and acting gains the form of an individual act, of a free act in the classical sense of the word.[34]

The prophetic dimension of Eatherly's act, then, lies in the determination with which he refused to be diverted from his sense of moral responsibility. He refused to submit to the apparatus which unless checked will so depersonalize the world that no one will be left to answer for its abuses. Nothing in fact will be left but "the charred land of the miserable and the radiantly clear conscience of the stupid." Thus Anders concludes:

By taking upon himself the guilt for the act of which he had only been a part, Eatherly is doing exactly the opposite—he attempts to keep conscience alive in the Age of Apparatus. And as conscience, by its very nature, is criticism, and criticism, by its very nature, non-conformist, he is being told: conscience is off-limits! [35]

4. THE PROPAGANDA OF IRRATIONALISM AND THE PORNOGRAPHY OF POWER

The consequence for Athenian culture of its failure to cope with internal social and intellectual crises was, as the Melian dialogue dramatically illustrates, a transition from the controlled and rational use of power as a means to an end, to what I shall hereafter refer to as the pornographic enjoyment of power for its own sake: a narcissistic indulgence whose ultimate passion is nothing less than the total annihilation of humanity and hence of the human race from the face of the earth. I doubt that we are any more protected than were the Athenians from the corruption that lies at the basis of our culture. Indeed, I must agree with the following statement by Henry Steele Commager:

It is three-quarters of a century now since Lord Acton made the famous pronouncement that all power tends to corrupt and that absolute power corrupts absolutely. We had thought, and hoped, that we were exempt from this rule, but it is clear that we are not. Power exposes us to the same temptation to ruthlessness, lawlessness, hypocrisy, and vanity to which all great powers were exposed in the past.

In a simpler day we could survive this threat of corruption without serious damage. We could count on wearing out the brief spell of violence and corruption, or on circumscribing its effects. But now that we are a world power and our conduct affects the fate of every nation of the globe, we can no longer afford this piece of self-indulgence. Now we must square our conduct with principles of law and of morality that will withstand the scrutiny of public opinion everywhere and the tests of history as well.[36]

But whether we can, as Commager urges us to, "square our conduct with principles of law and of morality that will withstand the scrutiny of public opinion everywhere and the tests of history as well"—an utterance which painfully parallels Pericles' remarks to his generation—depends upon how well we can cope with the propaganda of irrationalism that is growing in our society as it grew in Athens. In its most dangerous form, the propaganda of irrationalism brings about the substitution of the pseudo-morality of power and expediency for the genuine morality of honor and truthfulness. It is also the dynamism which feeds what Lewis Mumford has called "the forces of anti-life now swarming through our inner world, proclaiming that mechanical automation is superior to personal autonomy, that empty confusion is authentic design, that garbage is nourishing food, that bestiality and hate are the only honest expressions of the human spirit." [37] Irrationalism is an epidemic withering of belief in the obligation to think and to act in a systematic and orderly way. The epidemic, as Collingwood has pointed out, will express itself in every aspect of life. In education, for example, it manifests itself as the practice of favoring technical and vocational training and pretending that it is education; in religion it appears as a cult of emotion which in our own time has replaced the anguished and disciplined search for God. Infecting politics, it is the substitution of order for virtue, of emotional communion with a leader's thought for intelligent agreement with him, of conformity by terror for conformity by persuasion, of unpatriotic and treasonous activities for criticism and dissent.[38]

But let us suppose next that the tissues of the civilization invaded by this irrationalist disease are resisting it. The infection can thus progress only by concealing its true character behind a mask of conformity to the spirit of the civilization it is attacking. The attack will not succeed if the victim's suspicions are aroused. If you explicitly propose to abandon the ideals of justice and morality, you will lose your reputation with the persons you are trying to infect. But so long as nothing like a panic sets in, liberties can be taken which otherwise would not have any hope of succeeding. In short, let a sufficient number of men, whose intellectual respectability is vouched for by their reputations, pay sufficient lip service to the ideals of justice and morality, and they will be allowed to teach by example whatever kind of injustice and anti-morality they like, even if this involves a hardly disguised breach with the accepted canons of decency.

The ease with which this can be done will be much greater if it is done in a society dominated by a cult of abstract specialism, a cult whose distinguished lineage can be traced as far back as the Renaissance. By abstract specialism I mean both the idea that the study of any single subject can be carried out in isolation from every other subject, and the ideology already discussed that the scientific, philosophical, or intellectual pursuit of truth must be conducted in total indifference to its ethical implications. In a particularly eloquent passage written in 1923, Collingwood describes well this strange fruit of the Renaissance:

> In the first flush of that dawn, when art, religion, and thought, strengthened by their long medieval discipline of intimacy with each other, broke apart and suddenly began to work mir-

acles, men might be excused for thinking that in their separation lay the secret of their well-being. But the contrary soon appeared. Each cut off from the others tended more and more to lead its followers into some desert where the world of human life was lost, and the very motive for going on disappeared. Each tended to become a specialized activity pursued by specialists for the applause of specialists, useless to the rest of mankind and unsatisfying even to the specialist when he turned upon himself and asked why he was pursuing it. This is the point to which we have come today. . . . In the middle ages the artist was perhaps not much of an artist, the philosopher was by our standards only mildly philosophical, and the religious man not extremely religious; but they were all men, whole of heart and secure in their grasp of life. Today we can be as artistic, we can be as philosophical, we can be as religious as we please, but we cannot ever be men at all; we are wrecks and fragments of men, and we do not know where to take hold of life and how to begin looking for the happiness which we know we do not possess.[39]

The most damaging consequence of specialism is the reluctance of others to criticize the work of a specialist or to test his results and ideas by applying them to the actual practice of living. In that case, the agents of irrationalism can ensure immunity by putting forward their propaganda under the pretense that it is itself a special science which other specialists will understand that they must neither criticize nor subject to the test of lived experience. Irrationalism thus avails itself of the privileges accorded by a *rationalist* civilization in order to undermine the fabric of that civilization. Eventually, as we shall see, this kind of irrationalism will produce a total inversion of the moral order. Hitherto *praxis* was regarded as the servant of truth and morality. Gradually, however, the two were allowed to separate: morality and the pursuit of truth became indifferent to the practical needs of political action. And finally, the battle won, irrationalism celebrated in its victory by rejoining morality and action— but this time morality was placed in the service of action. Thus is born the cult of power, kept virile, as Julien Benda once explained, in his remarkable book *The Betrayal of the Intellectuals* (1927), by the intellectual pimps for power, the "clerks" (intellectuals, scientists, scholars, educators). Although the "clerks" continue to use the rhetoric of morality and the objective method, they have not only adopted the political passions of the goddess of power but are prepared even to sacrifice reason and intellect to the satisfaction of her needs, with the result that the forces that hitherto have saved mankind from self-destruction are now rendered impotent. Mankind has always been in the grip of the irrational. But, says Benda:

> thanks to the "clerks," humanity did evil for two thousand years, but honored good. This contradiction was an honor to the human species, and formed the rift whereby civilization slipped into the world.[40]

Today, however, these very same intellectuals have begun to betray their trust. No longer do they defend morality against politics. Intellectuals today have repudiated the spiritual values and have chosen instead the world, the flesh, and the devil. The new enemies of mankind are the Establishment intellectuals or realists who have become *moralists* of realism. It is one thing to admit with Machiavelli that morality and politics are simply indifferent to each other, and that sometimes one is forced into evil in order to pursue political goals; it is quite another matter, however, to rationalize one's evil acts in the name of an appropriate morality, to confuse the *expediency* of power with the *morality* of power. At least Machiavelli would admit that evil, even if it aids politics, still remains evil. But for the moralists of realism, as Benda portrays them, the act which serves the goals of power, regardless of its content, is invested with a moral character of its own by the mere fact that it does so. The evil which serves politics ceases to be evil and becomes good, and the *autonomy of morality* is thereby replaced by the *morality of power*.[41]

The most serious consequence of this spread of irrationalism will be the gradual acceptance of the dogma that for guidance in the practical problems of life, one must rely upon the advice of those who claim to be specialists on the one hand, but who are at the same time members of the power cult; whose advice, because it is part of a specialized science, must be accepted without criticism. To adapt a comment which Collingwood made about his own generation of Englishmen, but which captures the alarming plight of the present generation of Americans: if the leaders of America had wanted to train a generation of young persons expressly as the potential dupes of every adventurer in morals, politics, commerce, or religion, who should appeal to their emotions and promise them private gains which they neither could procure nor even meant to procure, no better way of doing it could have been discovered than the so-called "American Dream" with its appeal to the virtues of loyalty, patriotism, and allegiance to the authority of power.[42]

There are many reasons why our society has been so deeply affected by the disease of irrationalism. Commager traces such tendencies to certain nineteenth-century habits of brushing aside whatever was embarrassing, of taking for granted a double standard of history and morality: such as, for example, the conquest and decimation of the Indian—for, after all, Indians were only heathens. And when that argument lost its force, then, Commager continues, there were the undeniable charges that they got in the way of progress [43]—a point which I have already stressed in my Introduction. Susan Sontag also traces the irrationalist epidemic to the early genocidic tendencies of Americans. The early Americans, she writes,

> arrived in a country where the indigenous culture was simply the enemy and was in process of being ruthlessly annihilated, and where nature, too, was the enemy, a pristine force, unmodified by civilization, that is, by human wants, which had to be defeated. After America was "won," it was filled up by new generations of the poor, and built up according to the tawdry fantasy of the good life that culturally deprived, up-

rooted people might have at the beginning of the industrial era.[44]

The result, according to Miss Sontag, was that the dynamism of American life grew from an energy source that is simply pathological.

> Basically it is the energy of violence, of free-floating resentment and anxiety unleashed by chronic cultural dislocations which must be, for the most part, ferociously sublimated. This energy has mainly been sublimated into crude materialism and acquisitiveness. Into hectic philanthropy. Into benighted moral crusades, the most spectacular of which was Prohibition. Into an awesome talent for uglifying countryside and cities. Into the loquacity and torment of a minority of gadflies: artists, prophets, muckrakers, cranks, and nuts. And into self-punishing neuroses. But the naked violence keeps breaking through, throwing everything into question.[45]

To this must be added the apocalyptic phenomenon, characteristic of so many middle-class Americans, which Paul Goodman calls "privatism." [46] Driven by a crippling sense of powerlessness in a world which has lost all reason, one escapes into one's family, property, and the world of consumer goods, where there is still a possibility of exercising power and choice. Hence the almost pathological violence with which middle-class people tend to "cultivate their gardens," as it were. There is also the apocalyptic phenomenon of lawlessness which is becoming more and more of a national characteristic, its ultimate representation being the assassination of President Kennedy and the subsequent "public" execution of his "alleged" assassin who had been tried out of court by the judicial wisdom of the mass media. The filming of the actual events of this tragedy and the subsequent use of these films by the various news and television media was one of the most pornographic exploitations of violence in the history of man. And let us not forget the recent acceleration of techniques for the invasion of privacy, a scandal which is more and more becoming a subject for critical concern in America today. As Alan F. Westin has recently shown, in his book *Privacy and Freedom*, the ugly art of privacy-invasion has advanced further than most Americans probably realize:

> The effort to limit official surveillance over man's thoughts, speech, private acts, confidential communications, and group participation has for centuries been a central part of the struggle for liberty in Western society. This search for personal and group privacy has been waged against kings and legislatures; churches, guilds, manor lords, and corporations; sheriffs, welfare investigators, and political police. . . . [But] since World War II, spurred primarily by wartime development and government projects in the cold-war era, a series of scientific and technological advances has taken place that threatens the classic American equilibrium of privacy, disclosure, and surveillance. . . . A technological breakthrough in techniques of physical surveillance now makes it possible for government agents and private persons to penetrate the privacy of homes, offices, and vehicles; to survey individuals moving about in public places; and to monitor the basic channels of communication by telephone, telegraph, radio, television, and data line. Most of the "hardware" for this physical surveillance is cheap, readily available to the general public, relatively easy to install, and not presently illegal to own. . . . Further developments are possible that could pose wholly new and unprecedented intrusions into the emotions and mind of the citizen in the future. This technology has been developed at a time when socio-cultural changes in American life have produced an acceptance of these surveillance techniques by many private and public authorities, disseminating the new techniques rapidly through the society and outstripping the classic legal and social controls over "unreasonable" surveillance.[47]

No doubt many convincing arguments can be advanced to justify the need and usefulness of such devices in the control and ordering of society. But it is the merit of Professor Westin's book to expose the dangers inherent in the very

existence of these capabilities; the potentialities for the pornographic exploitation of such devices is almost beyond
calculation.

But finally, and most ominously, the energy of violence
expresses itself in the reckless pursuit of power, which is
justified, as was the genocide of the American Indian, in the
name of progress. And because this energy is, as Miss Sontag
says, "bad at its source," the pursuit of power is implicitly
pornographic, unleashing the repressed potentialities of man's
demonic nature and stimulating what might otherwise be
called an exercise of the "evil will." I do not know for *certain* whether man has such a nature as I ascribe to him in
this book. But that he is possessed of a capacity for evil I
have no doubt, and that he can celebrate in this evil as one
indulges one's appetites for pleasure—thus reinforcing his
satanic impulses—is to my mind an even greater cause for
concern.

And so we come back to the problems and questions raised
at the beginning: Who is man that he can both desire and
surrender his freedom? And what shall we do to be saved
from our present distresses? Collingwood's answer was that
the solution must come from a critical review of the chief
forms of human experience, a new treatise on human nature:
an enterprise which must be regarded not as a luxury or mere
amusement of a mind at leisure from more pressing occupa-
tions, but as a prime duty whose discharge is essential to the
maintenance not only of any particular form or type of
reason, but of reason itself. It is with the not very modest
intention of contributing to a new treatise on human nature
that the following pages are dedicated. The main theme of
this book, inadequate as it must seem to anyone with exacting
standards, is the mystery and outrage of man's capacity for
an enjoyment of evil and the ease and convenience with
which the exercise and experience of power can inadvertently
and surreptitiously contribute to that end.

CHAPTER TWO.
WHO IS MAN?
NATURAM SEQUERE!

Since our Moral sense represents Virtue as the greatest Happiness to the person possessed of it, our publick Affections will naturally make us desire the virtue of others.
Francis Hutchinson

Virtue belongs more to the savage than to the civilized man and vice owes its birth to society.
Count Buffon

Anyone who sets out to raise questions about man must be prepared to cope with the persuasive rhetoric of the skeptics and cynics who skillfully exploit the difficulty of the enterprise in order to further their own private ends. Philosophers like Socrates and Plato were among the first to suffer in this way. They recognized, as we also do, that a man's self-image is affected by the circumstances in which he finds himself: circumstances which are unstable, constantly changing, and infinitely variable. Some Greeks, notably the Sophists, declared simply that truth itself was relative, and that each man was himself the measure of this truth. The only thing men have in common, they would argue, is an innate capacity for aggression and a disposition to satisfy their appetites to the fullest. When it comes to a conflict between competing claims, there is only one court of appeal, namely, majority opinion or power backed up by force and coercion. Obviously, if we have no objective way of distinguishing truth from falsehood, then whether something is true and ought to be believed depends entirely upon who believes it and whether they have the power to back it up. In which case, the thing to do, if you want to influence the affairs of men, is not to be scientific and look for the so-called rational basis of truth; the more expedient course is first to gain power and then to master the techniques of persuasion—a thesis which can be verified simply by observing how men actually behave. In short, from the proposition "Truth is relative" we are led to the proposition "Might is right"—which exposes the kind of relation that exists between relativism and totalitarianism.

Against this kind of cynicism, philosophers like Socrates, Plato, and Aristotle contended not only that truth was objectively grounded but also that it could be the object of a special science. But whatever might be said about the character of this science, one thing was certain: it was not an *empirical* science. Plato, in fact, seemed to believe that the very idea of an empirical theory of values was a contradiction in terms—in the sense that it gives rise to the skepticism that it originally seeks to overcome. Naturally, since every man's experience is different, any attempt to generalize from this experience is bound to result in a chaos of confusions and conflicting opinions. Plato set out, therefore, to expose the fallacies of the empirical theory of man, and to replace it with a more acceptable rational or a priori theory.

The problem today is basically the same. We take experience more seriously than did the Greeks, but we are still looking for a touchstone with which to compare the various images of man described by contemporary thought. Anthropologists, for example, can tell us all about Western man, Zuni man, Bushman, European man, American man, middle-class man, and so on. But can they define universal man? Yet international relations demand that we agree on some set of standards to which men of all nations and races can appeal. We speak of international crimes against humanity, of international wars waged in the name of liberty, freedom, and justice, and so on. But how is it possible to go on believing this in the face of continuous efforts by cynical sophists to reduce morality to power? At least one solution, as I suggested in Chapter One, is to work toward the construction of a new treatise on human nature, which raises once again the question raised by Plato: Is there a universal a priori human nature underlying the behavioral differences which seem to divide cultures, societies, and even races?

To this question a variety of answers has been given, ranging from the theory of classical humanism, which says that human nature is intrinsically rational, to the theory of irrational man, which says that it is a law of nature that a man should satisfy his appetites to the fullest extent possible, even if this means gaining power over others. In the chapters to follow, I propose to discuss, and to some extent "live through," some representative examples of each of these views, beginning with the theories of rational humanism.

1. THE "FAITH" OF RATIONAL HUMANISM

In its most general form, rational humanism asserts that since man is basically good, the responsibility for any corruption of his behavior must lie with society. Corruption occurs whenever men are forced to behave against their real natures. Modern industrial society is a particularly corrupt state of affairs because it forces men to be ruthless, competitive, aggressive, and acquisitive in order to be successful. In a society such as ours, founded on an "achievement ethic," men are forced to compromise their humanity in order to succeed. But once we know what man really is, and what his real needs are, we need only reform society in order to eliminate the sources of evil and hence guarantee, within that society, the development of normal and happy individuals.

This view received much support during the seventeenth and eighteenth centuries, periods that historians have named "The Age of Reason" and "The Enlightenment," respectively. During the seventeenth century the spirit of humanism was alive in the writings of the Cambridge Platonists and certain Anglican divines. Writers like Benjamin Whichcote (1609–1683) and Nathaniel Culverwel (1618–1651), for example, argued that while men may conceivably possess a natural tendency to evil (which was usually thought to have its origin in the body), they possess an even more powerful disposition in the form of an innate moral sense which, once awakened, will overcome the body's natural tendencies to evil. To facilitate this self-actualization was the purpose of the revealed as well as the social law. If society is properly arranged, it will revive and awaken man's innate virtue and goodness and help him to overcome the less virtuous parts of his nature. What is more, they continued, it is only when man is virtuous that he is properly himself and hence happy. "Vice," said Whichcote, "is contrary to the Nature of Man, as Man: for it is contrary to the order of Reason, the peculiar and highest Principle in man." [1]

But of all the claims made by the exponents of seventeenth-century humanism, by far the most important was the suggestion that man's experience of virtue is accompanied by an experience of pleasure. Happiness, in other words, came to be defined in terms of feelings of sensuality. "There is no sensual Pleasure in the World," said Tillotson, "comparable to the Delight and Satisfaction that a good Man takes in doing good." And Richard Kidder wrote: "There is a Delight and Joy that Accompanies doing good, there is a kind of sensuality in it." [2]

During the eighteenth century this conception of virtue as an expression of man's natural passions was given further support by novelists and philosophers. There were, on the one hand, the popular portraits of the virtuous man of passion as represented in the novels of Samuel Richardson, Sir Richard Steele, and Laurence Sterne—the writers who, according to the literary critics, comprised the school of sentimentalism. At the same time there were the philosophical portraits drawn by the British philosophers Shaftesbury, Hutcheson, Hume, and Godwin, as well as by a host of French philosophers and intellectuals such as Buffon, Diderot, Rousseau, and Condorcet.

The first point made by these writers is that although man in the state of nature possesses an innate disposition to virtue, this disposition is easily corrupted by society. It is from society that man learns to be evil. Diderot's *Supplement to Bougainville's Voyage* (1772) is a classic statement of this view. "The life of savages," writes Diderot, "is so simple and our societies are such complicated machines."

> The [savage] is close to the origin of the world, while the European is close to its old age. The contrast between them and us is greater than the difference between a newborn baby and a doddering old man. They understand absolutely nothing about our manners or our laws, and they are bound to see in them

nothing but shackles disguised in a hundred different ways. Those shackles could only provoke the indignation and scorn of creatures in whom the most profound feeling is a love of liberty.[3]

Although Diderot is vehement in his indictment of society, he has little to contribute toward its eventual reform. Against the corruption of society he tends simply to extol the virtues of the state of nature. But in writers like Rousseau and Godwin, all of whom share Diderot's contempt for society as it presently exists, there is a further emphasis on the importance of social reforms, especially in politics and education. Providing society progresses along the right lines, wrote Godwin, the human condition can actually hope to become ideal. Since evil does not appear to arise out of the nature of man but only out of the institutions by which he has been corrupted, the salvation of man lies in social reform.

> Man is not originally vicious. . . . Simplify the social system, in the manner in which every motive, but those of usurpation and ambition, powerfully recommends; render the plain dictates of justice level to every capacity; remove the necessity of implicit faith; and we may expect the whole species to become reasonable and virtuous.[4]

The second main tenet of rational humanism, then, is the belief that the salvation of man is contingent upon the introduction of certain educational and social reforms. Given the proper social reforms, and the fact that nature has set no limit to the infinite perfectibility of man, rationalists like Condorcet looked forward to a future of immeasurable happiness and prosperity. To indulge in the contemplation of this prospect is for the philosopher (by whose efforts the progress of reason has been brought that much closer to fulfillment) a source of great comfort and pleasure. Such contemplation is in fact "an asylum."

> . . . there he lives in thought with man restored to his natural rights and dignity, forgets man tormented and corrupted by

greed, fear, or envy; there he lives with his peers in an Elysium created by reason and graced by the purest pleasures known to the love of mankind.[5]

Perhaps the most complex but intriguing of the French philosophers of the Enlightenment is Rousseau. What is interesting about Rousseau's thought is the way it develops from romanticism to positivism. In his early writings, such as *A Discourse on the Moral Effects of the Arts and Sciences* (1750), Rousseau declares himself the enemy of society and the champion of natural man. There is, he argues, a necessary connection between society and the imperfection of man. Progress has added nothing to our real happiness; it has only corrupted our morals.[6] Rousseau therefore conveys the impression that only the abolition of society and the return to nature can guarantee the survival of virtue in man.[7] In his more mature writings of 1762, however, such as *Emile* and *The Social Contract*, his views are considerably more sensible. He is still committed to the belief that men are born with a natural disposition to become good and to remain potentially good. The sentiment of justice, he declares throughout *Emile*, is "innate in the heart of man."

> There is . . . at the bottom of our hearts an innate principle of justice and virtue, by which we judge our own actions or those of others to be good and evil; and it is this principle I call conscience.[8]

What is more, if the life according to virtue and the pursuit of moral goodness is in accordance with our natures, then it follows that a man can be healthy in mind and body only when he is good. But Rousseau now argues that the corruption of man's behavior is due not to the effect of society as such but only to the effects of societies which are imperfectly designed; men become evil as a result of poor education. Given the right kind of education and the proper kind of society, it is not only possible but inevitable that man's natural capacity for goodness will prevail.

As in 1750, then, Rousseau is still committed to the importance of self-realization. But he now recognizes that it can be achieved only through the artful mediation of society. The salvation of man is not simply a matter of knowing oneself; it lies chiefly in the proper exercise of intelligence upon human nature. Without the mediation of education and society, man is bound to go astray; and this in spite of his natural capacity for goodness. Only society can save man from barbarism and savagery. Hence the emphasis must be upon a reform in the technology of education if men are to fulfill their true potentialities; it is not the abolition but the reform of society that is desired.

Indeed, so great is Rousseau's faith in the therapeutic and prophylactic powers of society in the production of virtue that he eventually describes the state as an institution for *forcing* men to be free. This is certainly a far cry from the almost anarchical qualities of his early thought. Liberty, he later contends, is obedience to the Law of Reason as embodied in social institutions, rather than to individual desire and caprice. More specifically, the task of education and law is *to train men to desire internally what they are forced by law to obey*. It is obedience to a self-imposed law of reason which ultimately, for Rousseau, defines the autonomy of the individual. And it is this concept of freedom and autonomy that forms the basis for the social contract.

> In order that the social compact may not be an empty formula, it tacitly includes the undertaking, which alone can give force to the rest, that whoever refuses to obey the general will shall be compelled to do so by the whole body. *This means nothing less than that he will be forced to be free.* . . .[9] What man loses by the social contract is his natural liberty. . . . what he gains is civil liberty. . . . [and] moral liberty, which alone makes him truly master of himself; for the mere impulse of appetite is slavery, while obedience to a law which we prescribe to ourselves is liberty.[10]

But although Rousseau speaks frequently of the law of reason, a careful reading of his works betrays the same sentimentalism that pervades the thought of almost every other seventeenth- and eighteenth-century thinker. In the end, as Pascal said, "the heart has its reasons which reason does not know. . . . We know truth not by reason but also by the heart, and it is this last way that we know first principles." [11] Thus Rousseau writes in *Emile* (Book Four):

> . . . such principles of conduct as . . . I must lay down for my guidance in the fulfillment of my destiny in this world, according to the purpose of my Maker. . . . I do not derive from the principles of the higher philosophy, I find them in the depths of my heart, traced by nature in characters which nothing can efface. I need only to consult myself with regard to what I wish to do; what I feel to be right is right, what I feel to be wrong is wrong. [12]

The decrees of conscience, in other words, "are not judgments but feelings," and "it is by these feelings alone that we perceive the fitness or unfitness of things in relation to ourselves, which leads us to seek or shun these things. . . . *To exist is to feel*." [13] And finally, in a statement which conveys the whole essence of romanticism, Rousseau declares:

> There is nothing sweeter than virtue . . . for what sweeter joy is there than this, to feel oneself a part of a system where all is good? [14]

This tendency to stress the importance of feelings rather than reason in the guidance of conduct, and to define conscience itself as an expression of feeling rather than an exercise of the intellect, is perhaps the most outstanding mark of Enlightenment humanism. For, as Rousseau puts it, to merely know the good is not to love it; it is only when by love we grasp what reason deems to be good that the power of conscience acts. To follow nature, then, means to follow human nature, the organic and primordial feelings of natural man, whose innate rationality will guarantee that once obstacles to the contrary have been removed, feeling will always guide men to the performance of reasonable and humane conduct. "He who obeys his conscience is following nature and he need not fear that he will go astray." [15]

Thus the message of classical humanism is twofold. From the romantic, sentimental side comes the dogma that man's inherent rationality is most perfectly exemplified in the disciplined expression of one's feelings and passions, while from the more positivistic side comes the theory that reason can flourish and the passions remain pure only in a properly designed society whose institutions and laws are in accordance with the true nature of man. The romantic strain is the origin of the hedonistic tendency to identify salvation with happiness and well-being, while the positivistic strain gives rise to the Utopian idea of salvation through social reform.

Both aspects are alive today. In spite of writers like Helvétius, Hobbes, Schopenhauer, and Freud, many contemporary social scientists and social critics continue to blame society or "the system" for man's imperfections. And in spite of Kierkegaard and Nietzsche there is still a tendency today to identify salvation with Utopia, happiness, and well-being. For those who accept society as the chief source of man's misery, the path to Utopia may lead through such diverse solutions as social freedom through rigid social control, on the one hand, and freedom through decentralization of control (in order to release natural impulses), on the other.

The contemporary version of humanism typically begins with a number of serious complaints, such as, for example, that our society, which believes one way and behaves another, has become corrupt, and youth, who represent for us the noble savage, are in revolt against this corruption. Through the revolt of the young, which is a perennial phenomenon, mankind encounters the stubborn resistance of human nature refusing to be compromised by philosophies of progress, conformity, and adjustment. Young people can no longer tolerate the Establishment apologists who decree that to be unhappy in a world that offers the greatest opportunities in the history of man is abnormal or pathological. How can you even begin to trust anyone who argues that our society is basically sound and that those who cannot reconcile themselves to it would profit more from psychoanalysis than social reform? And how much longer can we tolerate the nauseating spectacle of administrators, educators, and politicians, broadcasting from their pulpits through the megaphones of the mass media, about the opportunities, challenges, productivity, material standards, and achievements of our society? It is time that men asked themselves whether it is worth the human price we must pay for those accomplishments.[16]

All of this may be perfectly true, but I think it misses the mark. It fails to appreciate the possibility that society's restrictions on individuals, including all of the so-called corrupting influences, have their origin in man himself. Humanists talk about man's inhumanity toward man. But man's inhumanity is as much an expression of his human nature as is his humanity. Man, says Sartre, is the source of his own *négatité*.[17] Translated into moral terms, this means that man is the possibility of evil as well as of virtue.

This leads to a second reason for mistrusting humanism. If man is the being by whom *négatités* are disclosed in the world, then his condition is one of anguish. But humanism has equated virtue with happiness and well-being; or, at any rate, humanism has tended to defend a hedonistic interpretation of happiness. It is my view that either happiness is not the end of man or it cannot be equated with pleasure. The salvation of man lies not in complacency or well-being but in the assumption of responsibility—no easy matter. To suffer the burden of one's responsibility is neither a mere case of self-realization nor a question of forcing one's existence to coincide with one's essence. The anguish of responsibility lies in the need to wrestle with it in the face of evil. The freedom and salvation of man are accompanied not by feelings of sensuous delight but by an experience of dread which brings him to the very threshold of eternity only after having first charted a course through hell. The transcendence of evil cannot be separated from the journey through hell. The chief limitation of humanism is its failure to confront the dialectic of man's transcendence of evil through the experience of hell.

But in spite of its limitations, humanism carries a message of great importance. One of the most compelling critics of our time is Paul Goodman, who regards himself as a twentieth-century *philosophe* in the tradition of Diderot, Rousseau, and Voltaire. Goodman has repeatedly drawn attention to the discrepancy between the anti-humanistic ideology of "socialization," which defines the conditions leading to the healthy adjustment of man to his environment, and the ethic of "humanization," the cultivation and expression of man's basic nature. Is being socialized, asks Goodman, no matter what the society, the same as growing up and assimilating human culture? In his book *Growing up Absurd*, which has become a sort of bible for many of the young, Goodman gripes about the way the administrators of the twentieth century have hit on the theory that you can adapt people to anything if you use the right techniques.

Our social scientists have become so accustomed to the highly organized and by-and-large smoothly running society that they have begun to think that "social animal" means "harmonious belonging." . . . [I] take the opposite tack and ask, "Socialization to what? to what dominant society and available culture?" And once this question is asked, we must at once ask the other question, "Is the harmonious organization to which the youth are inadequately socialized, perhaps against human nature, or not worthy of human nature, and *therefore* there is difficulty in growing up?" If this is so, the disaffection of the young is profound, and it will not be finally redeemable by better techniques of socializing. Instead there will have to be changes in our society and its culture, so as to meet the appetites and capacities of human nature, in order to grow up. . . . *Growth like any ongoing function requires adequate objects in the environment* to meet the needs and capacities of the growing child, boy, youth, and young man, until he can better choose and make his own environment. . . . [But] our abundant society is at present simply deficient in many of the most elementary objective opportunities and worthwhile goals that could make growing up possible. It is lacking in enough man's work. It is lacking in honest public speech, and people are not taken seriously. It is lacking in the opportunity to be useful. It thwarts aptitude and creates stupidity. It corrupts ingenuous patriotism. It corrupts the fine arts. It shackles science. It dampens animal ardor. It discourages the religious convictions of Justification and Vocation and it dims the sense that there is a creation.[18]

The world that Goodman condemns is a world in which, as Yeats once said, "the best lack all conviction, while the worst are full of passionate intensity." It has no honor and no community. Goodman calls it an empty society:

I have singled out two trends of the dominant organization of American society, its increasing tendency to expand, meaninglessly, for its own sake, and its tendency to exclude human beings as useless. . . . Lack of meaning begins to occur when the immensely productive economy over-matures and lives by creating demand instead of meeting it. . . . Human beings tend to be excluded when a logistic style becomes universally pervasive, so that values and data that cannot be standardized and programmed are disregarded. . . . When there develops an establishment of managers and experts which deludes itself that it knows the only right method and is omnicompetent. . . .[19]

The chief conscious drive of the radical young is their morality. As Mike Harrington has put it, "they drive you crazy with their morality," since for it they disregard prudence and politics and they mercilessly condemn legitimate casuistry as if it were utterly phony. When politically minded student leaders, like—sometimes—the Students for Democratic Society, engage in "tactics" and the "art of the possible," they swiftly lose influence, whereas indignation or point of honor will rally the young in droves.

Partly *this drive to morality is the natural ingenuousness of youth freed of the role-playing and status-seeking of our society.* As aristocrats not driven by material or ulterior motives, they will budge for ideals or not at all.[20]

Goodman blames the loss of human happiness on the failure of socialization to accommodate the basic need of man to be involved in meaningful pursuits. His solution is to reform society in the direction of decentralization and to replace conformity with creative anarchy.

> I am . . . a community anarchist. I hold, for instance, that sovereign power must be diminished because it is too dangerous to live with; that people must be free of coercion in order to grow and adventure; that administration should be decentralized as much as possible, in order to multiply sources of initiative and experiment; and that there is a creative, a secure-making virtue in face-to-face association in urban and scientific societies.[21]

So far as the institutions of society are concerned, including the system of law and justice, as long as they offer means and opportunity for free action, they should be supported. But, he declares:

> When they become clogs and hindrances, and when their overwhelming drift is in the direction opposite from ours, for instance inevitably towards war, then we cannot cooperate with them or we must actively try to stop them or even to get them out of the way.[22]

Goodman's sole justification for rejecting unequivocal allegiance to the rule of law is that the law is servant to and not master of society; what is more, the society he lives in is his to alter as he chooses—so long, of course, as his conduct remains within the boundaries of decency and is what could be expected from any reasonable man threatened by the same circumstances.

> The government, the school board, the church, the university, the world of publishing and communications, are my agencies as a citizen. To the extent that they are *not* my agencies, at least open to my voice and action, I am entirely in revolutionary opposition to them and I think they should be wiped off the slate.[23]

The psychiatrist Robert Lindner was also alarmed by the widespread pressures in our society toward conformism. Lindner's point is that conformism breeds psychopathy. In America, the extent of conformism and its resulting psychopathy has reached epidemic proportions. The chief symptom of this growing disorder is the increasing presence among us of Mass Men and the rapid conversion of human individuals into a homogeneous Mass Manhood.

> The Mass man . . . is the psychopath *in excelsis*. A mechanized, robotized caricature of humanity, it is he who finally tears down around his own head the house of his culture. A slave in mind and body, whose life signifies no more than the instrument of his master's power, a lost creature without separate identity in the herding collectivity, a mindless integer of the pack who wakens from his torpor only when prodded by the whip from outside or the stab of brute appetite from within, it is he who finally inherits the earth and runs it to ruin. . . .
>
> Mass man, the universal psychopath, is born when the individual ego is weakened to the point at which it loses separate identity and is forced, for security, to merge with the mass. This becomes possible, however, only when what I believe to be a fundamental instinct of the human animal is outraged or betrayed. There is that within us that cannot be denied without destroying the essence of humanity. It is a drive to master, to overcome, to express positive protest against whatever stands in the way of the far-off, unknown goals of evolution. When this built-in urge is impeded or suppressed, the qualities that make up the humanity of man disappear, and in the place of man stands a goose-stepping automaton driven by animal lusts.[24]

Like Goodman, Lindner defines the essence of humanity as a rational potentiality to express oneself creatively, as an individual, as a rebel who seeks to progress through the critical transformation of values, standards, and institutions.

> Conformity is antibiological. Man cannot be denied his innate urge toward individuality. . . . When . . . he is given access to the fountainhead of his creativity—his distinction—he can contribute to the harmony created by the great human orchestra. Toward the re-establishment of the sacredness of human personality as a fact, then, our effort must be directed.[25]

I fully agree with this notion, but with some serious reservations. In addition to this Apollonian or virtuous capacity for goodness and creativity, and for rebelling against injustice and the arbitrary use of power, there is also in man a Dionysian or demonic capacity for aggression and for enjoying power, the expression of which is just as important as the expression of creativity. And this leaves us with the problem, as Freud well knew, of finding healthy, creative ways of expressing this aggression. In more concrete terms, the perennial problem of man is to build a world that is as much a home for the body as for the mind, as much a temple for the celebration of evil as for the celebration of good. To repeat a point already made: the salvation of man lies in neither the liberation of his inner nature nor in its repression but rather in man's ability to transcend that nature.

2. ANTI-HUMANISM AND THE IDEOLOGY OF ACHIEVEMENT AND SUCCESS

During the past few decades classical humanism has been increasingly challenged by certain neo-hedonistic theories of motivation, which in the best traditions of nineteenth-century liberalism emphasize the more aggressive tendencies in man but tend to define aggression in terms of achievement, and to define happiness as the satisfaction of the need for achievement. Some social scientists have even advanced the hypothesis that the economic growth and decline of Western culture is a function of variations in the "need for achievement" or "achievement motive" (not to be confused with the profit motive). Thus, much as Max Weber once argued that during the eighteenth century Protestantism supplied the motivation for the growth of capitalism, so it is argued today that the primary source of motivation is "the achievement ethic," "the irrational sense of having done [one's] job well." [26] But the suggestion is further made that this ideology has its origin in certain basic facts of human nature—in which case the very success of a culture must be measured by the degree to which it facilitates the expression of this need. According to the achievement ethic, the experience or sense of achieving is the source of meaning, while the material rewards that result through the satisfaction of that need are the sources of human happiness. Western cultures are therefore to be favored over non-Western ones, while within Western culture itself more importance is to be placed upon those institutions (such as "profit" and "property") that center on achievement and success than on those that do not. The inferiority of non-Western cultures is not a question of race but is due to the fact that these cultures inhibit the expression and systematic evolution of the universal capacity and need to acquire an achieving personality. Until these inhibiting factors are eliminated and replaced by new institutions and values which favor the development of an achieving personality, non-Western cultures cannot be expected to enjoy economic and technological progress. Such a view tends to support the pressures toward conformism as well as encourage the development of a technology of socialization which seeks to adjust the individual to the environment. But the humanist tradition argues the opposite thesis which stresses the adaptation of environment to the a priori needs of man.

The most articulate statement of the achievement ethic is the work of David McClelland. McClelland finds the source of the achievement ethic to be something which he calls "*n* Achievement," a psychological drive which under certain conditions gives rise to behavior exemplifying the achievement ethic. McClelland's chief interest, as an experimental scientist, is to locate and define the precise sources of high *n* Achievement.

> Why do some people have more *n* Achievement at some times than other people? Is it a question of racial heredity, challenge from the environment, or perhaps certain economic, political, or social disadvantages? [27]

McClelland's answer is, in effect, that *n* Achievement is essentially an acquired psychological drive which is reinforced (i.e., strengthened) through certain behavior patterns that are culturally based, such as, for example, "degree of challenge from the environment," "techniques of child-rearing practices" (especially with respect to "independence training"), "parent-child interaction," and "interaction of values, religion, and social class." [28] McClelland does not say that some people are by nature more adequately endowed than others with the capacity for achievement, but only that certain cultures have succeeded more than others in devising ways of reinforcing and strengthening this drive which every human being *qua* human being is potentially capable of attaining.

The most important cultural factor, according to McClelland, is the acquisition and modification of an achieving personality, which in turn derives from the socio-psychological structure of family relations. Man is as much a creator of his environment as he is the creature of it, and his responses depend as much on what he brings with him as on what the environment offers. [29] Every child, for example, enters his society with a quantum of initial *n* Achievement, depending on the nature of his early childhood experiences. If the child's initial motivation is high and if the environment is sufficiently stimulating (i.e., has the proper integration of values), the child will respond vigorously. But if the child is poorly motivated from the outset, if he does not have an achieving *personality* to begin with, he is not likely to respond to an achieving *society* no matter how stimulating and challenging it is. In short, says McClelland, "degree of challenge from the environment is an important determinant of aroused achievement motivation, but its effect is greatly influenced by initial levels of *n* Achievement" which originally derive from "certain beliefs and child-rearing practices in the family." [30] In addition to a technology of environmental design, McClelland therefore stresses the importance of a distinct, but not separate, technology of motivation and attitude arousal. And the latter amounts virtually to a technology of child-rearing practices which stresses early independence training.

On the basis of his experimental findings, McClelland then suggests various ways in which his theory of human nature can be applied to the engineering and control of society, with a view, of course, to accelerating economic growth by increasing *n* Achievement level. In particular, McClelland addresses himself to the following questions: What should be the psychological objectives of plans and policies aimed at accelerating economic development? What should an agency or a government do to speed economic growth in an under-developed country? [31] The point is not simply to shape an interesting and challenging environment but to shape an appropriate human nature to take advantage of that society. In summary form, this may be achieved by (a) replacing orientation toward tradition with "other-directedness" or "respect for the impersonal other"; (b) increasing the level of *n* Achievement through reforms in family and child-rearing practices, especially by decreasing the degree of father dominance; (c) introducing ideological "conversion" which "stresses individualistic achievement rather than passive dependency toward authoritarian forces beyond the individual's control"; (d) reorganizing fantasy life so that people motivate themselves by daydreaming about what they want to achieve; (e) utilizing existing *n* Achievement resources more efficiently, such as, for example, stimulating the emergence of a strong entrepreneurial class as well as a free-enterprise society within which to operate.[32]

What accounts for the rise in civilization? Not external resources (i.e., markets, minerals, trade routes, or factories), but the entrepreneurial spirit which exploits those resources—a spirit found most often among businessmen.

Who is ultimately responsible for the pace of economic growth in poor countries today? Not the economic planners or the politicians, but the executives whose drive (or lack of it) will determine whether the goals of the planners are fulfilled.

How can foreign aid be most efficiently used to help poor countries develop rapidly? Not by simply handing money over to their politicians or budget makers but by using it in ways that will select, encourage, and develop those of their business executives who have a vigorous entrepreneurial spirit or a strong drive for achievement.[33]

Enough! It is already clear that McClelland's liberalism is basically antihumanistic. It is governed by a set of values which will appeal only to those whose interests are best served by holding on to those values, namely, those who are members of the entrepreneurial or middle class. McClelland's theory of man, with its emphasis on the importance of ideology as a variable in the processes of social change, is itself a middle-class liberal ideology. It does not stress the more humanistic and personal goals of man: love, charity, aesthetic expression, intersubjectivity, and so on. It stresses instead the impersonal factor of achievement. McClelland's theories provide a formula for *Gesellschaft* rather than *Gemeinschaft*. A *Gesellschaft* is a mere "society" held together and regulated by rules and institutions to which its members are forced to conform. The efficiency of such a society depends upon the success with which individuals are adjusted, in the sense of being motivated to pursue the goals of that society. A *Gemeinschaft* is a "community" bound together by intersubjective relationships. In such a society a person's humanity, individuality, and interpersonal relationships are far more important than achievement and success. The achievement ethic, with its emphasis on the importance of phenomena which can be measured and manipulated, is therefore an ethic of technology and progress rather than an ethic of humanization. By contrast, the ethic of humanism is an ethic of love and intersubjectivity which stresses the importance of phenomena which cannot be measured and manipulated but which can only be "lived through," experienced, and shared—much as one experiences, enjoys, and shares a sunset. But of course such experiences do not lead to progress, social change, and economic advancement.

No wonder then that humanists like Paul Goodman and Edgar Z. Friedenberg are highly critical of the achievement ethic as a prescription for living. As Friedenberg puts it:

> The essence of our era is a kind of infidelity, a disciplined expediency. This expediency is not a breach of our tradition but its very core. And it keeps the young from getting much out of the diversity that our heterogeneous culture might otherwise provide them. This kind of expediency is built into the value structure of every technically developed open society; and it becomes most prevalent when the rewards of achievement in that society are most tempting. . . . Being different, notoriously, does not get you to the top. If individuals must believe that they are on their way there in order to preserve their self-esteem they will be under constant pressure . . . to repudiate the divergent elements of their character in order to make it under the terms common to mass culture. They choose the path most traveled by, and that makes all the difference. . . . For an adult this is self-destructive; for an adolescent it is the more pitiful and tragic, because the self that is abandoned is still immanent and further growth requires that it be nurtured and continuously clarified and refined. A pregnant woman may recover, more or less, from abortion; the fetus never does.[34]

The achievement ethic is an ideology of socialization which stresses the impersonal process through which an individual is shaped and trained to succeed in achieving the goals of his society. The humanist, on the other hand, is more interested in the dialectic of "humanization," the process through which a person learns simply to be an individual among others. But humanism is not really an alternative to the achievement ethic because basically it is addressed to an entirely different question. To prefer the ideology of humanism to the technology of achievement is not therefore to invalidate the former. It is simply to say that man's primordial, ontological need to be human takes priority over any such acquired need as n Achievement. A man may in fact be a "good achiever" (i.e., highly motivated and competent to pursue the goals of his society) and yet be bored with himself as a person. If he is a "poor achiever" but still accepts the basic values of his society, then he may regard himself as a failure. And if he is a poor achiever who at the same time rejects the values of his society, then he may become disengaged, as is obviously the case with the current generation of "hippies."

Finally, there is the inherent danger that since "achieving" and "succeeding" are experiences which necessarily point beyond themselves, the individual's expectation that hard work and dedication will eventually result in a real experience of accomplishment is bound to be disappointed. Nothing succeeds like success, but at the same time nothing else increases the appetite for more success. The more you succeed and the more you achieve, the greater your need for these experiences. And the greater your need, the less is the likelihood that you can ever be satisfied. The achieving society thus has the paradoxical but inevitable effect of producing its own downfall by converting man's primordial sense of potency into a desperate sense of impotency. The result is therefore a kind of "alienation," the alienation of man from himself and the alienation of man from society. But, as Goodman, Lindner, and others have argued, alienation is a potential source of violence. What begins, perhaps, as a protest against the threat to individual autonomy becomes in its own right a surrender of autonomy. And nothing is more potentially explosive than an individual who has lost his sense of autonomy and potency. It is the impotent man who, as Lindner puts it, "finally tears down around his own head the house of his culture."

3. ALIENATION AND THE PATHOLOGY OF VIOLENCE

The rising incidence of violence and psychopathy in our society has attracted the attention of almost every major social critic. Social pathology has become the most popular and lucrative academic enterprise of our time.[35] Erich Fromm was one of the first in the field with his book *The Sane Society*, published in 1955. In it he draws our attention to the discrepancy, so characteristic of modern industrial society, between material success, prosperity, and achievement, on the one hand, and human happiness, on the other. The aim of the whole socioeconomic development of the Western world, Fromm argues, is that of the materially comfortable life, relatively equal distribution of wealth, stable democracy, and peace, and the very countries which have come closest to this aim show the most severe signs of mental imbalance. These data raise a question in Fromm's mind as to whether there is not something fundamentally wrong with our way of life and its aims. Could it be, he asks, that the middle-class life of prosperity, while satisfying our material needs, leaves us with a feeling of intense boredom, and that suicide, alcoholism, and other forms of violence, such as crime and delinquency, are pathological ways to escape from boredom?[36]

The effects of conformism further stifle the creative expression of individuality. The whole of American culture is built upon the myth of individualism—but it is all a lie. The discrepancy between expectation and actual experience produces a psychological tension which is a potential source of violence. Unable to make one's presence felt in genuinely creative ways, the individual finds other means to assert himself, such as crime and, more recently, assassination.

The thesis that conformism and social alienation are primary sources of violence is one that must be taken seriously by Western society. For the individual unable to conform to the prescriptions of his society, there is always the retreat to anarchy, delinquency, and outright mutiny, while for the individual who has successfully internalized the propaganda of conformism there is the "paranoia" and violence of mass conformity, masquerading as patriotism and loyalty—as exemplified, for example, in the phenomena of racism, anti-communism, fulfilling "commitments" to "defend the freedom of less powerful nations," and crushing "riots"; phenomena which are intensified by the frustration of having been depersonalized and dehumanized. In short, to follow the arguments of Lindner, Fromm, and Goodman to their conclusions, when man's capacity to be creatively aggressive has been frustrated and blocked by the ideologies of conformity, adjustment, and achievement as a way of life, humanity becomes irrational, society totalitarian, and the exercise of power pornographic.

In such a society the rebellion of the young ceases to be a creative source of social change and becomes instead nihilistic, pathological, and mutinous. The result of the shift from creative rebellion to mutiny is the world of the emptied-out hipster, the rebel without a cause. In such a world, as Kenneth Rexroth once warned, there can be no true culture.

> The disengagement of the creator, who as creator is necessarily judge, is one thing, but the utter nihilism of the emptied-out hipster is another. What is going to come of an attitude like this? Is it possible to go on indefinitely saying: "I am proud to be a delinquent," without destroying all civilized values? Between such persons no true enduring interpersonal relationships can be built, and, of course, nothing resembling a true "culture"—an at-homeness of men with each other, their work, their loves, their environment. The end must be the desperation of shipwreck—the despair, the orgies, ultimately the cannibalism of a lost lifeboat. I believe that most of an entire generation will go to ruin—the ruin of Céline, Artaud, Rimbaud, voluntarily, even enthusiastically.[37]

This statement was truly prophetic. We have indeed borne witness to the ruin of a generation. The neo-hedonistic

Utopia driven by the achievement ethic has produced a society in which art and humanity itself have become meaningless and in which, as Rexroth complained, "it is impossible for an artist to remain true to himself as a man, let alone an artist." [38] But instead of simply withdrawing from the world to a position from which one could work toward its rejuvenation, the response has been nihilistic. During the forties and fifties there were hipsters and beatniks, and the sixties has produced hippies. These cults represent generations of young persons who, having been brought up under the achievement ethic, have rejected it by lapsing into nihilism. The style of this rejection is itself a symptom of a deeper impotency; it is a behavior of exhaustion. History has evolved three basic modes of revolt: rebellion, revolution, and mutiny. Rebellion brings into question specific values and institutions within a given system or social structure; revolution, on the other hand, seeks to replace the very system or structure itself; while mutiny is the sheer destruction of a system without alternatives to replace it. The alienated youth of our generation have lost faith in the effectiveness of either rebellion or revolution as forms of social change. As a result they have turned to mutiny, the only alternative left for those who wish to "howl" against society but who have lost patience with traditional modes of response. Mutiny is the last resource of the exhausted imagination. It is truly, as Rexroth says, "the desperation of shipwreck," the "cannibalism of a lost lifeboat."

One of the best insights into this phenomenon is John Clellon Holmes's novel *Go*, written in the fifties. Its theme is the "fatigue of too much society," or the pathology of achievement and success. Each of the heroes represents a typical pattern of alienation. The sense of the ultimate horror of the final apocalypse toward which the responses of alienated youth aspire is conveyed by the accidental death of one character, Agatson, under the wheels of a subway train.

Holmes's account of the world in which Agatson was driven to his death is profoundly revealing.

It is a wild world, inhabited by the lost, loveless, faithless, and homeless; a world of obscene drawings and humorless epigrams, whose walls are crowded with an illiterate testament to the bareness of the heart. In this world, lonely men scribble lewd invitations, frustrated tenderness becomes cruel with mockery, ungiven love becomes a vulgar obscenity. It is a world in which the ambitions of men have collapsed in a vision of unending lovelessness. To believe in this vision is to be outraged and to suffer the most unbearable of all losses, the death of hope. And when hope dies, there is only irony, a vicious, senseless irony that turns to the consuming desire to jeer, spit, curse, smash, and destroy. And so, says Stofsky, the poet, in a moment of prophecy: "The way to salvation is to die, give up, go mad. . . . To suffer everything. To be. To love . . . well, ruthlessly."

This is the world in which the poet Allen Ginsberg "saw the best minds of my generation destroyed by madness, starving hysterical, naked." Ginsberg poses the question we must all ask: "What sphinx of cement and aluminum bashed open their skulls and ate up their brains and imagination?" This is the question to which the poem *Howl* is addressed. And the answer, according to Ginsberg, is:

> Moloch! Solitude! Filth! Ugliness! Ashcans and unobtainable dollars! Children screaming under the stairways! Boys sobbing in armies! Old men weeping in the parks!
>
> Moloch! Moloch! Nightmare of Moloch! Moloch! the loveless! Mental Moloch! Moloch the heavy judger of men!
>
> Moloch! the incomprehensible prison! Moloch the crossbone soulless jailhouse and Congress of sorrows! Moloch whose buildings are judgment! Moloch the vast stone of war! Moloch the stunned governments.

Moloch! whose mind is pure machinery! Moloch whose blood
is running money! Moloch whose fingers are ten
armies. Moloch whose breast is a cannibal dynamo!
Moloch whose ear is a smoking tomb!

Moloch! whose eyes are a thousand blind windows! Moloch
whose skyscrapers stand in the long street like end-
less Jehovahs! Moloch whose factories dream and
croak in the fog! Moloch whose smokestacks and
antennae crown the cities!

Moloch is not simply materialism and social conformism. It
is the tyranny of an intellect driven by utilitarian goals seeking to rule over and depose the imagination. It may even be
the false humanistic belief that man is an angel who is led
astray by the apparatus and the machinery of society. Whatever it is, this much is clear: to stifle the imagination is to
violate the very nature of man. And this is why young men
in desperation must "burn for the ancient heavenly connection to the starry dynamos in the machinery of night."
Through uninhibited sensuality they seek to restore the fallen
imagination by which alone man can achieve oneness with
reality: The way to salvation, they say, is to encourage the
psychopath in oneself and to live in the enormous present
by engaging in every manner of drunkenness, dope addiction,
lewdness, and perversion, imaginable and unimaginable. But
herein lies the tragedy of hipsterism. In this attempt to
heighten the doors of perception through the systematic and
literal derangement of the senses, the hipster succeeds only in
destroying his potency forever. He comes to the end of feeling through feeling too much. The life of aesthetic distortion
dissipates into a life of sheer pornography. What begins as a
ritual of iconoclastic destruction ends in an orgy of aimless
insurrection. Mutiny is a pornographic form of rebellion because it is motivated by the sheer pursuit and enjoyment of
violence for its own sake.

Hipsterism is the path chosen by those who refuse to internalize the propaganda of conformism. The dialectic of hipsterism begins with a rejection of society which almost inevitably becomes a rejection of self. But, as we have noted, the same fate awaits even those who have made the adjustment to conformity as a way of life. Even the organization man, who tries to make love to society, suffers from a loss of self. His alienation is brilliantly portrayed in Robert Musil's novel *The Man Without Qualities*. If the hero of Holmes's novel, Agatson, represents the psychopath who has refused to conform, the hero of Musil's novel, Ulrich, represents the other dominant type of our time, the successful arch-conformist. The latter lives a surrogate existence at the level of accident and manipulation: a life totally depersonalized, totally devoid of responsibility. For a humanist like Musil, only a responsible self is a genuine self. A self without responsibility is *self-less*, that is to say, without qualities. But the organization man *is* such a soulless self. As Wylie Sypher puts it in his book *Loss of the Self in Modern Literature and Art*, the whole texture of his life is official, so official that his private self is only a hindrance to the larger operation of the policies he formulates.[39]

Musil's novel, like so much modern art and literature, is a study in the anonymous self, the self without meaning. Musil's hero says: "It's so easy to have the energy to act and so difficult to find a meaning for action," but the real terror of anonymity lies in its potential for apocalyptic madness. For implicit in the very awareness of the powerlessness and impotency that characterizes the loss of self, and from which the self desperately seeks to escape, is an almost uncontrollable appetite for power which then expresses itself in the most violent and irrational behavior. In short, the nothingness of anonymity is filled up by the pornographic pursuit of power. Captured and dominated by the "apparatus," the self *acts* but is no longer capable of *reaction;* one's acts are no longer "intended," no longer an expression or assertion of one's self. There is no longer any sense of self-fulfillment. And it is precisely this experience of "unfulfillment" which drives the self to selfhood through self-destruction.

The anguish of the unfulfilled self is the desire to coincide with itself, a feat which ironically can be achieved only in the loss of selfhood through nihilism. In Holmes's novel, the nonconformist is driven to nihilism when his nonconformity becomes pathological; the novel is therefore a study in the dehumanizing effects of making the struggle against evil the sole *raison d'être* of one's existence. In Musil's novel, the conformist is driven to nihilism through overidentification with role playing. In both cases there is a loss of the capacity to stand out as a person. The hipster suffers a loss of self when he substitutes acting out with others for suffering and feeling. The organization man loses his self through the substitution of pack-running and conformity for solitude. Neither the hipster nor the organization man is capable of real responsibility because neither is capable of suffering the outrage of injustice in silence.

In Dostoevsky's *The Brothers Karamazov*, Father Zossima makes a comment which conveys the whole essence of the humanist critique of society: "Fathers and teachers, I ponder 'What is hell?' I maintain that it is the suffering of being unable to love." [40]

The gist of the humanist complaint is that the society we live in is no longer adequate to the needs of man. What is more, since to live in our society is to violate the real essence of man's nature, the behavior of modern man has become pathological and hellish. In short, the tradition of humanism is based on the idea, as Erich Fromm puts it,

> that a sane society is that which corresponds to the needs of man—not necessarily to what he feels to be his needs, because even the most pathological aims can be felt subjectively as that which the person wants most; but to what his needs are *objectively*, as they can be ascertained by the study of man. [41]

The humanist is surely right to repudiate the theories of establishment sociology and to protest the vindication of aggression, anonymity, conformity, and depersonalization in the name of progress and economic "success." But to object to these abuses in the name of a doctrine which defines man as a being whose very essence is to love and cooperate with others will, I fear, produce the same disappointment as the attempt to live according to the achievement ethic. For to argue, as humanists are prone to, that man is basically humane, and that he becomes irrational only when his human nature is violated by a corrupt society, is precisely the faith that the study of man has brought into question. The claim that irrationality is in large part a response to the corruption within society is true enough, but to assert that the latter is the sole cause of the former is surely misleading.

Even Fromm himself recognizes, in *Escape from Freedom*, that in addition to the desire for freedom there is also, at the very center of man's being, an innate *fear of freedom*, an instinctive wish for submission, which can become a source of irrational behavior.[42] Of course, Fromm does not himself go far enough with this hypothesis, for in the end even the so-called instinctive fear of freedom turns out to be a result of the social process of which man is the product.[43] But the question I am raising, and which must be faced squarely if the science of man is to enjoy authenticity, is whether the culture, of which man is the product, is not itself grounded in certain primordial dispositions which, far from being merely acquired, tend to resist change. What if man's capacity for evil is an essential rather than an accidental or acquired part of his nature? What if his very capacity to love and create depends upon how he "lives through" and assimilates his primordial urge to murder and destroy? What if good and evil, rather than being opposites, are in fact dialectical partners? It will not do simply to obscure man's capacity for radical evil by redefining it as a need for achievement. But neither will it do to pretend that no such need exists. The point is neither to accommodate evil nor to ignore it, but to transcend it. It is the transcendence of evil which concerns us here. And I am suggesting that it is only when man learns how to celebrate in and ritualize his primordial disposition to evil that he can transcend it. To transcend evil means to have first lived through it—which is why the history of man, what we learn from it, and how we live it over again, is so vitally important to man's future salvation.

There is, however, a further point to the humanist critique of society with which I would wholeheartedly agree. It is that, for whatever reasons, modern man has been so violated that he is virtually looking for an excuse to go mad, and he will seize every opportunity to do so. And, of course, if the customer wants to go mad, the agents of progress are only too willing to comply and provide such opportunities. This complaint forms the basis of a recent attack by Lewis Mumford on American car manufacturers, a complaint which strikes deep into the pathology of our culture.

> As if to show their contempt for the whole safety argument, the manufacturers have lately souped up their cars and their advertising slogans in order to appeal to the least safe group of motor car drivers, the newly licensed adolescents and the perpetual adolescents; and they have underlined their inducement to calculated recklessness by giving the cars appropriate names, Thunderbirds, Wildcats, Tempests, Furies, to emphasize hellbent power and aggressiveness, while their allies in the oil industry, for good measure, offer to place a tiger in the tank. Speed is the pep pill that the motor car manufacturers are now cannily offering to adolescents like any dope peddler; and since power and speed are both regarded as absolute goods by the worshippers of the Sacred Cow, both as good in themselves and as the surest way to expand the industry and maximize the profits, why should anyone suppose that any other human considerations will modify their homicidal incitements? Speed, marijuana, heroin, and lysergic acid are all attempts to

use a scientific technology to overcome the existential nausea that the lopsided development of this very technology is the main cause of. . . . In short, the crimes and the misdemeanors of the motor car manufacturers are significant, not because they are exceptional but because they are typical. . . . The insolence of the Detroit chariotmakers and the masochistic submissiveness of the American consumer are symptoms of a larger disorder: a society that is no longer rooted in the complex realities of an organic and personal world; a society made in the image of machines, by machines, for machines; a society in which any form of delinquency or criminality may be practiced, from meretriciously designed motor cars to insufficiently tested wonder drugs to the wholesale distribution of narcotics and printed pornography, provided that the profits sufficiently justify their exploitation. If those remain the premises of the Great Society we shall never be out of danger —and never really alive.[44]

4. MARXISM AND THE REVOLT AGAINST BOURGEOIS REASON

Finally, the humanist critique of society may be compared with the various neo-Marxist critiques, which may be summed up as follows. In a capitalist society such as ours, driven by a profit motive, all of man's creative talents are corrupted. Reason gives way to practical intelligence, the capacity to maximize one's advantages in the struggle for existence. Science is pressed into the service of technology. Social science becomes the "mistress" of motivation research and personnel management. And art, language, color, and sound are degraded into instruments of advertising. The result is that human rationality inevitably becomes crippled, and progress toward human happiness is replaced by the enjoyment of power among those who make up the ruling classes. In any capitalist society, the underdog becomes more and more alienated from the goals of his society, and he soon becomes an easy prey to the forces of irrationalism.

For example, the comman man revolts against the bourgeois

ethic and the rationale of capitalism. But his revolt soon becomes a revolt against reason itself and turns into anti-
intellectualism, lawlessness, and crime. It is tempting, of
course, says the Marxist, to interpret such behavior as an
expression of an instinct to aggression, as Freud suggests. But,
the Marxist insists, irrational behavior is not an expression
of innate aggression; it testifies rather to the refusal of man
to accept the corrupt rationality of capitalism. The revolt
against reason that characterizes our time is a revolt against a
capitalist rationality which has pressed reason into the service of a marketplace society—from which it follows, according to the Marxist, that the structure of that society must be
reformed rather than anything in human nature. Capitalism
must be replaced by socialism, and private property, the instrument of aggression, must be abolished.

One leading Marxist, Paul Baran, compares the proletarian
outcry against bourgeois rationality with Dostoevsky's "Underground Man" who "vomits up reason" in order to show
his disgust for society.[45] This irrational outburst is the only
reaction available to the isolated and helpless individual who
is being crushed by a corrupt society. And so, Baran says,
it is profoundly right. But what Baran fails to realize is that
Dostoevsky's Underground Man is not driven to irrationality
by a pernicious social order alone. He is driven to his aggressive behavior by the very Dionysian, irrational forces that
Marxists like Baran fail to recognize, driven by his very
nature to vomit up any and every attempt to rationalize him.
He would be just as disgusted by the so-called open and
cooperative society of Marxism as by the closed, competitive
society of the bourgeois world. If the analogy between the
proletarian revolt and Dostoevsky's Underground Man is to
be maintained at all, then it introduces factors that neither
humanists nor neo-Marxists are equipped to deal with.

5. QUO VADIMUS: ANARCHY OR SOCIAL CONTROL?

The case against modern industrial society can hardly be more eloquently summed up than in the following outcry by Professor Burris, the hero of B. F. Skinner's Utopian novel, *Walden II.*

> A golden age, whether of art or music or science or peace or plenty, is out of reach of our economic and governmental techniques. Something may be done by accident, as it has from time to time in the past, but not by deliberate intent. At this very moment enormous numbers of intelligent men and women of good will are trying to build a better world. But problems are born faster than they can be solved. Our civilization is running away like a frightened horse, her flanks flashing with sweat, her nostrils breathing a frothy mist, and as she runs, her speed and her panic increase together. As for your politicians, your professors, your writers—let them wave their arms and shout wildly as they will. They can't bring the frantic beast under control.[46]

But what is to be done about all this? What do the critics recommend as solutions to our problems? Paul Goodman favors a program of anarchy, creative disorder, and civil disobedience as the only means through which society can be rehumanized. Goodman believes that these expressions of populism are far preferable to the anomie and crime that result from attempting to conform to a corrupt society. Robert Lindner offers us a "prescription for rebellion," an invitation to resist every effort to make us conform before it is too late. In stunning contrast to the proposals of Goodman and Lindner, Kenneth Rexroth and the friends of the Beat generation have defended a policy of creative disengagement, a quiet withdrawal from society into a life of meditation. While Erich Fromm talks about the therapy of love and productive labor. And Skinner, who represents the cool voice of behavioral science, rejects all humanistic solutions in favor of a scientifically based program of social control:

> The danger of the misuse of power is possibly greater than ever. It is not allayed by disguising the facts. We cannot make wise decisions if we continue to pretend that human behavior is not controlled, or if we refuse to engage in control when valuable results might be forthcoming. . . . We are all controlled by part of the world in which we live, and part of that world has been and will be controlled by men. The question is this: Are we to be controlled by accident, by tyrants, or by ourselves in effective cultural design? [47]

The voice of rational humanism, then, as represented by critics like Goodman, Lindner, and Erich Fromm, together with the neo-Marxists, friends of the Beat generation, and the liberal behaviorists like McClelland and Skinner, share in common what strikes me as an incomplete view of human nature. Let me make it clear, however, that my complaint with humanism and liberalism is not that they are lacking in depth and profundity. On the contrary, what humanists from Diderot to Goodman have had to say about society is both compelling and incisive. And there is even much of value in the liberalism of a B. F. Skinner. Nor am I complaining about the fact that the liberal and humanist concepts of man have not yet been given empirical proof. Indeed, I would contend that the concept of man at issue here is not one for which the ordinary empirical techniques of verification are even relevant. The humanist and liberal conceptions of man are presuppositions which function like myths and are applied to the hermeneutic (i.e., interpretative) "understanding" of experience. Likewise, the concept of man that underlies the exposition of my own argument is also a presupposition or a myth. As opposed to a "causal" or "scientific" analysis of behavior, which seeks primarily to *explain* particular events by subsuming them under empirically verifiable laws, a hermeneutic analysis seeks rather to disclose the subjective significance or "meaning" of human behavior. Thus, for example, a phenomenon like "emotion" can be traced to its social, psychological, and metabolistic causes, in which case it is treated as an effect or consequence. Or else it can be hermeneutically interpreted as a mode whereby the human subject escapes from a difficult situation by magically endowing the world with the very qualities necessary to justify his behavior. Is my anger *a result* of a provocation, or do I become angry *in order to* be provoked; do I hate you *because* you are hateful, or have you become hateful to me *in order that* I may hate you? As Sartre has argued, the substitution of *in order to* for *because* (or as a result of) is a matter of the utmost importance.[48] It illustrates once again the difference between the phenomenological approach, which is essentially hermeneutic and which seeks to disclose the human significance of a phenomenon, and the naturalistic approach, which is essentially causal-explanatory.

The validity of a hermeneutic interpretation of lived-experience, then, is not contingent upon the amount of empirical proof that can be assembled in its favor. It depends rather on its success (admittedly a subjective criterion) in explaining the existential structure of our lived-experience, thus providing a conceptual framework for understanding the social world.[49] Because the chief weakness of rational humanism, as I have come to understand it, is its inadequate treatment of the irrationality and absurdity of the human condition, the following chapters will be devoted to a discussion of the implications of some of the theories which have developed in opposition to the theories of liberalism and rational humanism.

According to the mythology of rational humanism, men consciously pursue goals that are inconsistent with their unconscious, natural needs for rationality and love. As a result they are driven to the unnatural behavior of aggression and violence. But the responsibility for this corruption lies chiefly with society. The solution is to reform society so as to liberate man's natural capacity for goodness and thus facilitate the need for man's social existence to coincide with his essence. The mythology of irrationalism, however, argues that while the *precipitating* cause of violence and pathological behavior may lie in the structure of society, the *predisposing* cause lies deep within the nature of man himself. Irrational behavior, in other words, is just as natural as rational behavior. What is more, it is self-regulating and self-reinforcing. Because it is natural and satisfies a natural urge, it cannot be easily eliminated. The solution is to reform society in order to control rather than to liberate natural man. Man's social existence, far from coinciding with his essence, seeks rather to reconcile the opposing forces within his nature— even if this involves a repression of the irrational.

Against these fundamental mythologies I will outline a somewhat different one which represents man as an ambivalent consciousness which seeks both *to-be-what-it-is-not* and *not-to-be-what-it-is*. Or, to put it another way, man's very being compels him both to negate and to transcend himself. Indeed it is only by negating himself that he can transcend himself. It will be my contention, however, that this transcendence is not accomplished through the application of techniques of social control which seek primarily to reconcile opposing forces within human nature. The mode of transcendence is essentially an act of the imagination. First man must transcend himself through the imagination; only then can he give himself over to the reform of society. To attempt the latter without the former is like attempting to drive an engine without fuel. It simply will not work.

CHAPTER THREE.
TWILIGHT OF
THE IDOLS:
IRRATIONALISM
AND THE
EVOCATION
OF EVIL

You cannot play with the animal in you without becoming wholly animal, play with falsehood without forfeiting your right to truth, play with cruelty without losing your sensitivity of mind. He who wants to keep his garden tidy doesn't reserve a plot for weeds.
Dag Hammarskjöld

Man is neither angel nor brute, and the unfortunate thing is that he who would act the angel acts the brute.
Pascal

In the year 1882 the prophet Zarathustra emerged from the imagination of Friedrich Nietzsche to become a prodigious event in the intellectual history of European consciousness. Zarathustra was a madman who came uninvited into the streets and churches of Europe to intone his unforgettable requiem on the death of God, and promise of the eternal recurrence of man's solitude and despair with all the agonies of his tormented body and soul.

Where is God? I mean to tell you. *We have killed him*—you and I! We are all his murderers! But how have we done it? How were we able to drink up the sea? Who gave us the sponge to wipe away the whole horizon? What did we do when we loosened this earth from its sun? Whither does it now move? Whither do we move? Away from all suns? Do we not dash on unceasingly? Backwards, sideways, forwards, in all directions? Is there still an above and below? Do we not stray as through infinite nothingness? Does not empty space breathe upon us? Has it not become colder? Does not night come on continually, darker and darker? Shall we not have to light lanterns in the morning? Do we not hear the noise of the gravediggers who are burying God? Do we not smell the divine putrefaction?—for even Gods putrefy! God is dead! God remains dead! And we have killed him! How shall we console ourselves, the most murderous of all murderers? The holiest and the mightiest that the world has hitherto possessed has bled to death under our knife—who will wipe the blood from us? With what water could we cleanse ourselves? What lustrums, what sacred games shall we have to devise? Is not the magnitude of the deed too great for us? Shall we not ourselves have to become Gods, merely to seem worthy of it? There never was a greater event—and on account of it, all who are born after us belong to a higher history than any history hitherto! [1]

The words of the uncanny visitor fell on ears that listened but were not able to hear. The nineteenth century had not yet outgrown the Age of Reason. Men still clung to their weak-willed beliefs in progress and the infinite perfectibility of man. And so the madman, having intoned his *requiem aeternam deo*, smashed his lantern to the ground and cried:

> I come too early. I am not yet at the right time. This event is still on its way, and is traveling. It has not yet reached men's ears. Lightning and thunder need time, the light of the stars needs time, deeds need time, even after they are done, to be seen and heard. This deed is as yet further from them than the furthest star, *and yet they have done it*. What are these churches now if they are not the tombs and monuments of God? [2]

The prophet was right. Generations were yet to come before the death of God would become an experience for all men. It is an experience that began as early as the Renaissance but needed many centuries of stony sleep before it would finally come home to roost. The death of God was first plotted when Copernicus and Galileo deprived man of the belief that his world was the center of the universe. Then Darwin robbed man of his peculiar privilege of having been specially created, by relegating him to a descent from the animal world. Man, said Darwin, is the product of natural selection. His being here is a sheer accident, and with all his noble achievements, with sympathy which feels for the most debased, with his godlike intellect which has penetrated into the secrets of nature, with all these exalted powers, man still bears in his bodily frame the indelible stamp of his lowly origin.[3] But the most bitter blow of all came from Freud, who crushed what remained of the ego's naive self-love by declaring to a generation already unnerved by the impact of the Darwinian revolution that the ego is not master in his own house but is subject to the play of unconscious and irrational forces.[4] Think now what it means to find out that history and nature do not work acording to pre-existing purposes but by natural selection, that the actions of men are

directed not by reason but by irrational forces in the unconscious, and that the order of society is grounded not in
divinely created goals but in the simple necessity to repress
the irrational in order to survive. How long would it be, then,
until even normal men would begin to suffer the death-of-
God experience that Nietzsche reserved only for madmen
and prophets?

It was not long after Nietzsche's death that the sages of the
twentieth century began proclaiming from their own lips
that God is dead and man must give up the illusion of immortality, for so long as he lives by this illusion, man is nothing but a useless passion. As early as 1901, Bertrand Russell
exposed the outlines of the universe as seen through the eyes
of modern science, thus making the anxieties of the inquisitors who hounded Copernicus and Galileo come true:

> That man is the product of causes which had no prevision of
> the end they were achieving; that his origin, his growth, his
> hopes and fears, his loves and his beliefs, are but the outcome
> of accidental collocations of atoms; that no fire, no heroism,
> no intensity of thought and feeling, can preserve an individual
> life beyond the grave; that all the labors of the ages, all the
> devotion, all the inspiration, all the noonday brightness of
> human genius, are destined to extinction in the vast death of
> the solar system, and that the whole temple of man's achieve-
> ments must inevitably be buried beneath the debris of a uni-
> verse in ruins—all these things, if not quite beyond dispute, are
> yet so nearly certain, that no philosophy which rejects them
> can hope to stand. Only within the scaffolding of these truths,
> only on the firm foundation of unyielding despair, can the
> soul's habitation be safely built.[5]

Some years later, the American historian Carl Becker re-
peated these sentiments in a statement that catches even more
of the spirit of modern thinking and exposes further the
sources of our anxiety.

> Edit and interpret the conclusions of modern science as ten-
> derly as we like, it is still quite impossible for us to regard man

as the child of God for whom the earth was created as a temporary habitation. Rather must we regard him as little more than a chance deposit on the surface of the world, carelessly thrown up between two ice ages by the same forces that rust iron and ripen corn. . . . What is man that the electron should be mindful of him! Man is but a foundling in the cosmos, abandoned by the forces that created him. Unparented, unassisted, and undirected by omniscient or benevolent authority, he must fend for himself, and with the aid of his own limited intelligence find his way about in an indifferent universe.[6]

But now that the false idols have been removed and the doors of perception cleansed, so that man can finally discover who he is, then what? The most important result of the death-of-God experience is the removal of the forces that had restrained man's irrational appetites. Hitherto men were sustained by the illusion that they had been specially created. But the modern world has replaced the old mythologies with the new myth of man as a chance product of nature. And so man now finds himself on the other side of despair. Once again the demonic breaks through to shatter the Apollonian vision, and twenty centuries of playing at being human are vexed to nightmare by the angry voice of the irrational, now liberated and never again to be silenced. The future of man, as Nietzsche and Freud well knew, would depend upon how he wrestles with the thrust of the demonic.

2. IRRATIONALISM AND THE NEW PORTRAIT OF MAN

This portrait of man as a creature of unreason comes at a time when men have already begun to doubt the truth of the humanist theory of rational man. The idea that evil owes its origin to man himself is far from being a radically new idea. To begin with, the concept of human nature corrupted by sin goes back to the birth of Christianity, while the recognition of man's capacity for evil is a cardinal doctrine of the Old Testament. Furthermore, the irrationality of man in the state of nature as opposed to the rationality of his social existence has long been a distinction of importance for political philosophers. The classic description of man in the state of nature is *The Leviathan* by Thomas Hobbes, published in 1651:

> [In the state of nature] . . . the life of man [is] solitary, poor, nasty, brutish and short . . . [In] this war of every man against every man . . . nothing can be unjust [because nothing can be just]. The notions of right and wrong, justice and injustice, have there no place . . . Force and fraud are in war the two cardinal virtues . . . In such a condition every man has a right to everything; even to one another's body.[7]

During the eighteenth century, this view was supported by writers like Helvétius, Mandeville and La Rochefoucauld. Mandeville's critique of Shaftesbury sums up well the attitude of those who regard self-interest rather than an innate moral sense to be the essence of human nature. Shaftesbury, Mandeville complains,

> imagines that men, without any trouble or violence upon themselves, may be naturally virtuous. He seems to require and expect goodness in his species, as we do a sweet taste in grapes and China oranges, of which, if any of them are sour, we boldly pronounce that they are not come to that perfection their nature is capable of. . . . This noble writer . . . fancies that as a man is made for society, so he ought to be born with a kind of affection to the whole, of which he is a part, and a propensity to seek the welfare of it.[8]

Against this Mandeville argues

> not only that the good and available qualities of men are not those that make him beyond other animals a social creature, but, moreover, that it would be utterly impossible either to raise any multitudes into a populous, rich, and flourishing nation, or when so raised, to keep and maintain them in that condition without the assistance of what we call Evil, both natural and moral.[9]

But the sentiments underlying the attack on humanism received their most eloquent and rhetorical expression in the *Maxims* of La Rochefoucauld. "Our virtues," La Rochefoucauld declared, "are but vices in disguise." The following are typical expressions of the romantic cynicism which La Rochefoucauld elevated into a popular entertainment.

> Self-interest to which are ascribed all our crimes should frequently be given the credit for our good deeds.
>
> For most men the love of justice is only the fear of suffering injustice.
>
> If we master our passions it is due to their weakness, not our strength.
>
> No man should be praised for his goodness if he lacks the strength to be bad: in such cases goodness is usually only the effect of indolence or impotence of will.
>
> Moderation has been elevated into a virtue in order to curb the ambitions of the great and to console the second-rate for their lack of good fortune and the mediocrity of their talents.[10]

But whereas La Rochefoucauld's cynicism was primarily a style of wit which had no other purpose than to shatter the mindless complacency and smugness of middle-class morality, the irrationalism of Hobbes, Helvétius, and Mandeville formed a basis from which to construct a positive theory of social reform. Against the humanists, who derive order from the pre-existing virtues of man in the state of nature, irrationalists believe that virtue is a derivative of order, which in turn depends upon a technology for controlling the irrational. For realists like Hobbes and Freud, the irrationality of man is a sufficient justification for the use of power to legislate virtue into existence. For, as Freud puts it in *Civilization and Its Discontents* (1930):

> Men are not gentle, friendly creatures wishing for love, who simply defend themselves if they are attacked . . . a powerful measure of desire for aggression has to be reckoned as part of their intrinsic instinctual endowment. The result is that their

neighbor is to them not only a possible helper or sexual object, but also someone who tempts them to satisfy their aggressiveness on him, to exploit his capacity for work without compensation, to use him sexually without his consent, to seize his possessions, to humiliate him, to cause him pain, to torture and to kill him. *Homo homini lupus.* Who, in the face of all his experience of life and history, will have the courage to dispute this assertion? As a rule this cruel aggressiveness waits for some provocation or puts itself at the service of some other purpose, whose goal might also have been reached by milder measures. In circumstances that are favorable to it, when the mental counter-forces which ordinarily inhibit it are out of action, it also manifests itself spontaneously and reveals man as a savage beast to whom consideration towards his own kind is something alien. . . . The existence of this inclination to aggression, which we can detect in ourselves and justly presume to be in others, is the factor which disturbs our relations with our neighbor and which makes it necessary for culture to institute its highest demands.[11]

On the basis of this concept of natural man as a thoroughly irrational being, there have developed throughout the course of Western intellectual history two separate traditions. The first, which I call the "philosophy of romantic individualism" or "the ethic of power," says that while the state of nature is characterized by a war of all with all, it is also a law of nature that the strong shall prevail over the weak. The implication of this view is a state of moral anarchy. The second tradition argues that in order to save ourselves from the cannibalism and moral anarchy that inevitably result from men being left in the state of nature, we need a system of controls to insure the survival of all. This is one source of what has come to be known as the contract theory of society, according to which morality is defined by its usefulness in maintaining social order.

Of course, both of these theories, the philosophy of heroic individualism and the contract theory of society, *insofar as they pretend to be ethical theories,* are logically invalid. For as ethical theories they commit the fallacy of deriving the "ought" from the "is," of deriving normative statements from purely descriptive statements. There is no logic which states that because man *is* basically irrational, he *ought* therefore to live a life of irrationality or he *ought* to submit to the terms of the contract. Nothing in fact follows except that a man is free either to resign himself to what he is, and passively submit himself to his irrational nature, or else to revolt against his nature by coming to terms with it and thereby transcending it. Either way it is man's own choice.

Yet, in spite of the logical confusions upon which it is based, the unqualified theory of irrational man is believed by many to be true and to imply certain things about how we ought to act. For this reason it must be taken seriously, especially with respect to the psychological issues involved and the moral recommendations that typically follow.

3. THE PHILOSOPHY OF ROMANTIC INDIVIDUALISM AND THE ETHIC OF POWER

According to the philosophy of romantic individualism (which is by far the more nihilistic of the two views), since it is a law of nature that the strong shall prevail over the weak, it follows that men ought to assert themselves as vigorously as possible, and may the best man win. But as most men are weaklings and would easily be subdued by the heroic few, they have banded together, in the name of something called justice, to prevent the strong from gaining the upper hand. And so virtue is really nothing more than a rationalization of the inability, among those who hold power, to compete with those who by the grace of nature are more adequately endowed. Underlying this attitude is the cynical belief that every man, including the most virtuous, bible-thumping defenders of justice and righteousness, will satisfy his evil impulses if he thinks he can get away with it. Men pretend that they do the right things because they are right;

in fact, they do these things under compulsion and only because they are unable to do wrong.

The force of this cynicism is well expressed in the famous story of the ring of Gyges, which Plato tells in Book One of the *Republic*. Imagine, says Plato, that a just man has suddenly acquired a ring which gives him the power to make himself invisible. Not even the most just of men would have such iron strength of will as to stick to what is right and keep his hands off other people's property. For he would be able to steal from the shops whatever he wanted without fear of detection, to go into any man's house and seduce his wife, to murder or to release from prison anyone he felt inclined to, and generally to behave as if he had supernatural powers. And in all this the just man would in no way differ from the unjust.

Plato rightly regarded this kind of cynicism as a serious threat to the survival of human culture, and he devoted much of his time to refuting it. But before refuting it he tried first to understand it, and he therefore allowed those who held it to state their case as forcefully as possible. This he did through the explosive speeches of some of his leading characters: Thrasymachus in Book One of the *Republic* and Callicles in the dialogue called *Gorgias*. Callicles' version of it is especially forceful and deserves serious attention.[12]

Generally speaking, says Callicles, nature and convention are inconsistent with one another. Conventions concerning what is right and wrong are made by the weaklings who happen to form the majority of mankind. But such values are established only with respect to the self-interest of these same weaklings and are entirely inconsistent with the true law of nature which states that right is the superior ruling over the inferior, and that a man ought to encourage his appetites to be as strong as possible instead of repressing them. In Freud's language, Callicles is declaring that "where *Ego* now reigns there should *Id* be."

For the majority, of course, this is an impossible ideal. And that is the real reason why any attempt to gain an advantage over the majority is said to be wrong and base, and men call it criminal. What is more, in order to ensure their own survival, the weaklings praise the ideology of moderation and righteousness, which they elevate to the rank of the highest virtue, and then force young men of superior quality to guide their lives by it. Thus the society of weaklings destroys the possibility of genuine individualism by setting up a dictatorship of mediocrity. Young men of superior character are taken from youth, subjected to a course of charms and spells (such as religion), and enslaved by the repetition of the dogma that all men are created equal, and that equality is fine and right. The truth is, of course, that in an endeavor to conceal their own weakness they blame the minority whom they are ashamed of not being able to imitate, and maintain that the real virtues of the heroic individual who lives by nature are in fact evil and wrong: for make no mistake, even the inferior and weak have the same desires and lusts as the superior and strong, and it is only because of their own lack of manliness, and because they are unable to satisfy their own passions, that they praise moderation and righteousness. In other words, says Callicles, *all men who speak of virtue do so only because they are themselves too weak to be evil.*

But, says Callicles prophetically, the reign of mediocrity will not last forever. There will come a day when the heroic individual will achieve his vengeance against the society of weaklings; there shall arise men sufficiently endowed by nature to shake off and break through and escape from the chains of mediocrity: men who will tread underfoot our texts and our spells, our incantations and unnatural laws, and by an act of revolt reveal themselves, in the full blaze of the light of natural justice, masters instead of slaves.

Thus did Callicles, in the fourth century B.C., expound the eschatology of heroic individualism—and I am reminded of a poem by W. B. Yeats, made all the more terrifying when regarded in the light of Callicles' prophecy.

Turning and turning in the widening gyre
The falcon cannot hear the falconer;
Things fall apart; the center cannot hold;
Mere anarchy is loosed upon the world,
The blood-dimmed tide is loosed, and everywhere
The ceremony of innocence is drowned;
The best lack all conviction, while the worst
Are full of passionate intensity.

Surely some revelation is at hand;
Surely the second coming is at hand.
The second coming! Hardly are those words out
When a vast image out of *Spiritus Mundi*
Troubles my sight: somewhere in the sands of the desert
A shape of lion body and the head of a man,
A gaze blank and pitiless as the sun,
Is moving its slow thighs, while all about it
Reel shadows of the indignant desert birds.
The darkness drops again; but now I know
That twenty centuries of stony sleep
Were vexed to nightmare by a rocking cradle,
And what rough beast, its hour come round at last,
Slouches towards Bethlehem to be born? [13]

The philosophy of romantic individualism is based on the proposition that man is a thoroughly irrational creature, dictated by lust and self-interest, destined to be sacrificed to an eternal struggle in which only the fit can survive. This notion has been stated and restated in one form or another throughout the centuries. It has always been the subject of a great deal of literary exploration—especially in the contemporary literature of violence and the theatre of the absurd, which confront us with dramatic images of modern man's odyssey of self-destruction. A most compelling literary expression of this view can be found in Rex Warner's novel *The Professor*, written in 1938. In it, the agent of irrationalism is a young man called Julius Vander, who is ironically portrayed as the Professor's own protégé—which is, I suppose, the author's way of drawing attention to the claim that the responsibility for the rise of evil in the world often lies with the so-called custodians of virtue.

In one very powerful scene, the Professor, who represents the tradition of naive humanism, is confronted by Vander, the new Prometheus, who lectures him on the real basis of morality and on the consequences of having repressed man's natural instinct for aggression in the name of the artificial morality manufactured by the tradition of humanism.

The origin of all morality, says Vander, is the instinct for self-preservation, which includes the instinct to preserve everything that one has identified with oneself. Its chief emotional stimuli are hatred and fear. Its intellectual stimulus is always the desire to receive some advantage. Even the so-called fellow feeling, which is the source of conventional morality, derives from this natural source: for in the end, morals, virtues, and conventions are just another way of asserting the advantage of the majority. What humanists and Christians call the universal and natural law of justice and love is really no more than a convenient way for those in power to protect their own interests. Such notions as God and the divine right of kings, for example, are designed for internal consumption primarily as a means of keeping people within a society in their right places. This is why conventional morality is always being modified and changed.

Real morality, however, does not change. Its roots in human nature are too deep. It springs from the ineradicable desires of the human body, blood, bone, and senses. It has the force of an instinct—the instinct to preserve and amplify one's life. It therefore has more in common with hatred than with love. It is, in its perfect form, the morality of the proud and lonely individual. Real morality is the pride of man in himself, in his possessions, and in the power he can exercise over others. This is the deepest thing in man; it has always been so and always will be so. But artificial morality has

ignored this basic law of nature and for this reason is destined
to fail. And if it does fail, its failure will be due as much to
the hypocrisy of those who defend it as to the fact that it
ignores the basic law of human nature. For the preachers
of conventional morality have never themselves attempted to
behave according to their own doctrines; perhaps if they had,
human nature might indeed have undergone some slight
change or modification. Instead, the exponents of virtue have
constantly repressed men's natural instinct for lust and hatred
and self-preservation in the name of a morality which they
openly violate—and because this fact is obvious to all concerned, it has fostered in the deep places of the souls of the
masses such bitter hatred for humanistic Christian culture and
religion that Christians and humanists would tremble if they
knew the fraction of it.

The trouble with you is that you are no psychologists, and
that is why we shall smash you. . . . For we appeal not to the
intellect, or even to immediate self-interest, but to the dark,
unsatisfied, and raging impulses of the real man. It is we who
are, in a psychological sense, the liberators. The only freedom
that you offer is economic freedom, a barren and dusty slogan
which no one who is not an intellectual even understands.

So I say that where you preach abstract universal love we
shall restore the polarity without which no emotion is more
than the shadow of a thought. We shall be united in our
hatred for those who love indiscriminately. Where you emphasize the unique value of the individual as a devoted servant
in some sort of incomprehensible anthill, we shall give real
individuals the right either to lead or to follow, and in both
cases to keep their integrity and self-respect. When in your
sickly hypocrisy you talk of understanding and tolerance we
shall understand but not tolerate. We shall give to man the
satisfaction to which he is entitled, the satisfaction of striking
down his enemies like rats. And since the basis of our action
is, unlike yours, psychologically sound, the masses of the people will like it. They are sick and tired of you and of your

ways of thought, and in one moment all their enforced respect and complacency will turn to the vast relief of the practical enjoyment of hatred.[14]

This is a clear statement of the philosophy of romantic individualism or the ethic of power. Power is defined not simply as an evil means which is reluctantly employed for the sake of a greater good, but as something to be enjoyed for its own sake, which is sheer pornography. But the apotheosis of what I mean by the pornography of power is O'Brien's speech to Winston Smith at the end of Orwell's *1984*.

The party seeks power entirely for its own sake. We are not interested in the good of others; we are interested solely in power. Not wealth or luxury or long life or happiness; only power, pure power. What pure power means you will understand presently. We are different from all the oligarchies of the past in that we know what we are doing. All the others, even those who resembled ourselves, were cowards and hypocrites. The German Nazis and the Russian Communists came very close to us in their methods, but they never had the courage to recognize their own motives. They pretended, perhaps they even believed, that they had seized power unwillingly and for a limited time, and that just round the corner there lay a paradise where human beings would be free and equal. We are not like that. We know that no one ever seizes power with the intention of relinquishing it. Power is not a means; it is an end. One does not relinquish a dictatorship in order to safeguard a revolution; one makes the revolution in order to establish the dictatorship. The object of persecution is persecution. The object of torture is torture. The object of power is power.[15]

O'Brien is making a claim that none of us today can afford to ignore. We are a part of a society which has achieved absolute power. And now we are engaged in using that power in order to defend our freedom from communist aggression. Our leaders tell us, as the leaders of Athens told them, that we use our power reluctantly. O'Brien claims that though we may deceive ourselves into believing this, the truth is that we have come to enjoy power for its own sake. If we really believed in the priority of virtue over power, we would do something about eliminating the conditions that force us to the reluctant use of power. In fact, our efforts seem always to achieve the opposite goal. And so O'Brien leaves us with the following questions: Do we use our might in places like Vietnam in order to protect freedom and to curb aggression from alien and hostile forces, or have we surreptitiously engineered a threat to freedom and do we stimulate aggression in order to be in places like Vietnam and to use our power reluctantly? Do the leaders of American society employ power merely as an instrument through which they hope eventually to eliminate the conditions which occasion such uses of power in the first place, or have they fallen under the spell of power, perhaps to the point of forming a power cult, dedicated to the worship of power for its own sake? The communists, of course, must ask themselves this same question. Now I must confess that I do not know the answer; nor does anyone else I know of. But it seems to me that we had better start finding out, and soon.

There is another point to O'Brien's eulogy on power, which is even more frightening. Once we realize that power is always enjoyed for its own sake, we also realize that the ultimate goal of power is not power over matter or over things but power over human beings, over the body and above all over the mind. Real progress is the successful creation of institutions through which men can openly celebrate in their bestiality.

The real power, the power we have to fight for night and day, is . . . power . . . over men. . . . How does one man assert his power over another . . . ? By making him suffer. Obedience is not enough. Unless he is suffering, how can you be sure that he is obeying your will and not his own? Power is in inflicting pain and humiliation. Power is in tearing human minds to pieces and putting them together again in new shapes of your own choosing. Do you begin to see then, what kind of a world we are creating? It is the exact opposite of the stupid hedonistic utopias that the old reformers imagined. A world of fear and treachery and torment, a world of trampling and being trampled upon, a world which will grow not less but *more* merciless as it refines itself. Progress in our world will be progress towards more pain. The old civilizations claimed that they were founded on love and justice. Ours is founded upon hatred. In our world there will be no emotions except fear, rage, triumph, and self-abasement. Everything else we shall destroy—everything. Already we are breaking down the habits of thought which have survived from before the Revolution. We have cut the links between child and parents, and between man and man, and between man and woman. No one dares trust a child or a wife or a friend any longer. . . . There will be no loyalty except loyalty towards the Party. There will be no love except the love of Big Brother. There will be no laughter except the laugh of triumph over a defeated enemy. There will be no art, no literature, no science. . . . There will be no distinction between beauty and ugliness. There will be no curiosity, no enjoyment of the process of life. All competing pleasures will be destroyed. But always—do not forget this—always there will be the intoxication of power, constantly increasing and constantly growing subtler. Always, at every moment, there will be the thrill of victory, the sensation of trampling on an enemy who is helpless. If you want a picture of the future, imagine a boot stamping on a human face—forever.[16]

In each of the preceeding eulogies on power, the one by Julius Vander, from Rex Warner's novel *The Professor*, and the one by O'Brien, from George Orwell's novel *1984*, questions of great urgency are raised. In each case the charge is made that the pornographic enjoyment of power is a consequence, first of all, of an excessive repression of man's irrational, Dionysian, and demonic nature (which is a direct result of the influence of rational humanism). But secondly, and more importantly, the point is made that the cult of power is strongly reinforced by the perennially widespread hypocrisy of pretending, on the one hand, that we human beings are basically good and virtuous while all the time indulging ourselves in behavior which is in fact contrary to this belief. Men who play with power under the pretense that it is only a temporary expedient are simply providing their unconscious aggressions with weapons not likely to be easily surrendered. The use of power as a means, and the propaganda of irrationalism which comes to the defense of this expediency, leads inevitably to the cult of power and the pornographic enjoyment of power for its own sake.

In Robert Louis Stevenson's masterful study of the ambivalence of human nature, *Dr. Jekyll and Mr. Hyde,* Dr. Jekyll, the humanist, originally creates Mr. Hyde (in itself a thoroughly evil act) so that the forces of evil incarnated in Hyde can be scientifically studied and eventually banished from the human psyche. So confident is Jekyll in the iron strength of his own virtue that he sincerely believes he can give birth to evil without being corrupted by it. But alas, the virtuous Jekyll is no match for the satanic Hyde: once the demon has been released, the angel seeks every excuse to descend himself into the depths of depravity. Hyde takes possession of Jekyll and the two are destroyed together. The tragedy of Dr. Jekyll lies in his naive confidence that the irrational can be totally eliminated or repressed. The moral of the story, if indeed there is one, is surely that to attempt the total elimination of the irrational is as absurd as pretending that it does not even exist. Both illusions rest on an incredible and fantastic trust in the efficacy and incorruptibility of human virtue. And so, the critics of rational humanism would seem to be saying, *for God's sake let us stop pretending that we are angels or we shall surely become devils!*

CHAPTER FOUR. IRRATIONALISM AND THE INVOCATION OF VIRTUE

The second half of the twentieth century may be remembered for its solution of a curious problem. Although Western democracy created the conditions responsible for the rise of modern science, it is now evident that it may never fully profit from that achievement. The so-called "democratic philosophy" of human behavior to which it also gave rise is increasingly in conflict with the application of the methods of science to human affairs. Unless this conflict is somehow resolved, the ultimate goals of democracy may be long deferred.

B. F. Skinner

I have distinguished two types of irrationalism. The first, which I call the philosophy of romantic individualism, says that while the state of nature is characterized by a war of all with all, it is also a law of nature that the strong shall prevail over the weak. The most dramatic expression of this view is the pornographic enjoyment of power for its own sake. And I have asked whether this perversion is not a direct consequence of pretending to be virtuous, on the one hand, while at the same time behaving contrary to this pretense and then rationalizing this behavior with clever theories about the expediency of power and its reluctant employment as a means for the realization of cherished goals. I have also suggested that this duplicity is at least partly a result of the fact that men are not angels who are led astray by the influences of society but have as part of their very being a powerful drive toward aggression. Until this basic irrationality can find its needed forms of expression, its effect on society will continue to be destructive rather than creative.

1. SOCIAL CONTROL AND THE EXORCISM OF EVIL

The second type of irrationalism, which I will call "pragmatic irrationalism," is precisely the attempt to define the conditions under which man's basic irrationality can be both controlled and creatively expressed. In contrast to humanism, pragmatic irrationalism argues that the basis of order is not virtue but that virtue derives from order—which in turn derives its justification from the success with which it is able to control human nature. The natural instincts of men are to inflict wrong or injury and to avoid suffering it. Experience has shown, however, that the disadvantages of suffering it far exceed the advantages of inflicting it. Men therefore agreed to make a contract with each other in order to avoid the consequences of the war of all with all which characterizes the state of nature. In order to secure this contract, they proceeded to make laws which they called "right" and "just," and in order to ensure that they would be obeyed, the laws were proclaimed to be sanctioned by morality and divine will. The truth is, however, that virtue is only a useful expedient which men tolerate simply as a defense against the possibility of mutual destruction.

The irrationalist version of the contract theory of society is one of the oldest and most seriously debated of the various doctrines that have influenced the direction of Western political thought. Plato describes it as "the common opinion of the nature and origin of justice" and contrasts it to the philosopher's attempt to ground justice in a system of eternal truths.[1] For Plato, pragmatism was by definition a non-philosophical attitude toward the world. Beginning with the Renaissance, however, pragmatism or political realism becomes the only reasonable choice for the philosophers. The famous advice of Machiavelli (1469–1527) that "the end justifies the means" introduces a new era in political philosophy.[2] The significance of Machiavelli's thought lies in his decisive separation of politics and morality. Political progress is achieved not through the pursuit of moral ideals but by force and fraud. Not morality but expediency is the source of political wisdom. Even when one does good, it is only for profit. The ideal prince, for example, is one who knows how to combine the lion and the fox, to be a man toward his friends and a beast toward his enemies. Therefore, a prudent prince ought not to "keep faith" when by so doing it would be against his interests and when the reasons which made him bind himself no longer exist. Of course, Machiavelli confesses, "If men were all good, this precept would not be a good one; but as they are bad, and would not observe their faith with you, so you are not bound to keep faith with them." Nevertheless, he adds, in the end one's success depends not so much on one's skill in the art of deception as on one's ability to disguise one's deception. Men are always ready and willing to be deceived providing it is done with sufficient grace and artistry. But, above all, the prince "must have a mind disposed to adapt itself according to the winds, and as the variations of fortune dictate, and . . . not deviate from what is good if possible, but be able to do evil if constrained." [3] Thus Machiavelli writes in his *History of Florence* (1525), in a passage which is put into the mouth of one of the most fiery and experienced of the plebian leaders during the revolt of 1378:

> . . . I am very sorry to hear that many of you, for reasons of conscience, repent of the things you have done and wish to refrain from anything more; if it is true, you certainly are not the men I believed you were. Neither conscience nor ill fame ought to frighten you, for those who conquer, in whatever way they conquer, never because of it come to disgrace. Of conscience we need take no account, for when people fear hunger and prison, as we do, they cannot and should not have any fear of Hell.
>
> If you will observe the way in which men act, you will see that those who attain great riches and great power have attained them either by fraud or force; those things, then, that they have snatched with trickery or with violence, in order to conceal the ugliness of their acquisition, under the false title of profit they make honorable. But those who, through either lack of prudence or great folly, avoid these ways, always are smothered in servitude and poverty, for faithful servants are always servants, and good men are always poor; none come out of servitude except the unfaithful and the bold, and out of poverty except the rapacious and fraudulent. God and nature have put all men's fortunes in their midst, and these fortunes are more open to stealing than to labor, and to bad rather than good arts. From this it comes that men devour one another; and they who are weakest always come off worst. We ought, then, to use force when we get a chance. [4]

By the seventeenth century both the wisdom of Machiavelli and at least some version of the contract theory of society finds it way into the main body of almost every major political theory. Hitherto, only Sophists and demagogues dared to speak this way. Now, even the philosophers argue the merits of pragmatism and political realism: Thus, Thomas Hobbes, the greatest political philosopher of the age, declares unequivocally that:

> The final cause, end, or design of men, who naturally love liberty and dominion over others, is the introduction of that restraint upon themselves, in which we see them live in commonwealths, is the foresight of their own preservation, and of a more contented life thereby; that is to say, of getting themselves out from that miserable condition of war, which is necessarily consequent, as hath been shown, to the natural passions of men, when there is no visible power to keep them in awe, and tie them by fear of punishment to the performance of their covenants, and observation of the laws of nature. . . . For the laws of nature, as *justice, equity, modesty, mercy,* . . . of themselves, without the terror of some power, to cause them to be observed, are contrary to our natural passions, that carry us to partiality, pride, revenge, and the like. And covenants, without the sword, are but words, and of no strength to secure a man at all.[5]

There is a difference, of course, between Hobbes and Machiavelli. Machiavelli writes in an age that has not yet achieved political order, and his thought takes the form, therefore, of a manifesto whereby order can be restored through the seizure of power. The point of his advice is that power can be secured only by following the law of nature itself. The key to political success lies not in suppressing but in exploiting the state of nature. By contrast, Hobbes writes in an age that has already witnessed a seizure of absolute power but that is now being threatened by a wave of populism which seeks a more democratic society in accordance with man's natural rights—which presupposes an entirely different conception of the state of nature. Hobbes therefore attempts a defense of the status quo by demonstrating what could happen if men were to return to the state of nature. And he hopes in this way to demonstrate why it is better to place power in the hands of an absolute monarch who alone transcends the limitations of the human condition. But on the question of human nature itself, both Machiavelli and Hobbes draw the same portrait, and Hobbes's apology for absolutism is the sequel to Machiavelli's manifesto for the actual seizure of power which is but the first step toward the establishment of an absolute state. It is because of man's irrational nature that Machiavelli recommends the tactics he does with respect to the seizure of power, and that Hobbes recommends the use of force and punishment for the subsequent control of society by those who have gained power.

During the eighteenth century, the irrationalist version of the contract theory found support in the thought of Claude Adrien Helvétius (1715–1771), who is, incidentally, one of the most ignored political theorists of all time. Although Helvétius accepts the Hobbesian view of man in the state of nature, he manages to arrive at a somewhat different conclusion than did Hobbes concerning the best and wisest means for achieving political order. For Hobbes, the fact of man's irrationality justifies the maximum degree of repression. The best way to ensure the survival of virtue and justice is to punish vice and injustice. In contemporary psychological jargon, Hobbes's theory of social control is based on a technology of negative reinforcement. For Helvétius, however, the fact of man's irrationality requires a much different solution. Given the fact that man is driven primarily by self-interest toward the pursuit of pleasure and the avoidance of pain, the art of good government ought to consist of techniques for educating the individual to desire the general good or to seek pleasure through the performance of virtuous acts.

> . . . the science of education may be reduced perhaps to the placing of man in that situation which will force him to attain the talents and virtues required of him . . .[6]

It is only by good laws that we can form virtuous men. All

the art therefore of the legislator consists in forcing them by self-love to be always just to each other. Now, in order to compose such laws, it is necessary that the human heart should be known, and in the first place, that we should be convinced that men having sensibility for themselves, and indifference with respect to others, are neither good nor bad, but ready to be either, according as a common interest unites or divides them; that self-love, a sensation necessary to the preservation of the species, is engraved by Nature in a manner not to be erased; that a physical sensibility has produced in us a love of pleasure and a hatred of pain; that pleasure and pain have at length produced and opened in all hearts the buds of self-love, which by unfolding themselves give birth to the passions, whence spring all our virtues and vices.[7]

The point of education, in other words, is not to force men to virtue solely as a means of avoiding punishment; it is rather to persuade men to virtue by rewarding the performance of virtuous acts. Or, to put it once again into the language of contemporary psychology, the art of government is based on a technology of positive reinforcement. If society is wisely ordered, then men may be conditioned to satisfy their love-of-self through the acquisition of attitudes and the performance of acts that directly exemplify the virtues—which is a much wiser course than forcing them to virtue only as a means of avoiding the pain of punishment that follows the performance of vicious acts.

Thus did Helvétius, by a somewhat different route, arrive at precisely the same conclusion reached by Rousseau. For although Rousseau's view of man in the state of nature is vastly different from Helvétius' view, yet both agree in the end that the aim of education is to force men to desire and to choose to do what they are in fact compelled by law to do if society is to be just and orderly. But—and this is where the two philosophers differ in their interpretations of what is being accomplished—whereas Rousseau would regard this state of affairs as one in which men are permitted to fulfill their inherent capacity to live the virtuous life, for Helvétius the sole motivation for human conduct is self-interest. For Rousseau, the happiness of living according to the rule of law and of submitting oneself to the general will is a genuinely moral experience. For Helvétius, happiness is nothing more than the pleasure that accompanies the expression of self-interest. As the latter can be satisfied in any number of ways, it is the task of politics and education to manipulate the environment in such a way as to maximize the coincidence between self-interest and the general good.

One of the most recent defenses of the irrationalist version of the contract theory is to be found in the writings of Sigmund Freud, who makes it the basis for a psychoanalytic theory of culture and social control. According to Freud, the contract marks a decisive step in the evolution of culture. It symbolizes the victory of society over the single individual, and the renunciation (within the psychological makeup of the single individual) of the instinct for aggression in favor of a social conscience.[8] But, says Freud, while the real causes of our obeying the laws of society are pragmatic rather than ethical, it is sometimes useful to sustain the illusion that our behavior is governed by ethical and religious considerations. What is more, in order to distract ourselves from the irrational urges of our unconscious, society must provide a variety of creative outlets which will enable us to be aggressive without being destructive. Creativity is a primary source of the forms through which aggression can be usefully employed.

It was for this reason that Freud strongly opposed the Marxist doctrine that society rather than human nature is the source of aggression. Against the Marxists, Freud argues that capitalism is a desirable form of social order because it permits the expression of native aggression by displacing and sublimating this aggression into socially acceptable forms of behavior, such as competing for money, status, and power. Thus Freud declares in *Civilization and Its Discontents:*

The communists believe they have found a way of delivering us from evil. Man is wholeheartedly good and friendly to his neighbor, they say, but the system of private property gives power to the individual and thence the temptation arises to ill-treat his neighbor; the man who is excluded from the possession of property is obliged to rebel in hostility against the oppressor. If private property were abolished, all valuables held in common, and all allowed to share in the enjoyment of them, ill-will and enmity would disappear from among men. Since all needs would be satisfied, no one would have any reason to regard another as an enemy; all would willingly undertake the work which is necessary. I have no concern with any economic criticisms of the communistic system; I cannot enquire into whether the abolition of private property is advantageous and expedient. But I am able to recognize that psychologically it is founded on an untenable illusion. By abolishing private property one deprives the human love of aggression of one of its instruments, a strong one undoubtedly, but assuredly not the strongest. It in no way alters the individual differences in power and influence which are turned by aggressiveness to its own use, nor does it change the nature of the instinct in any way.[9]

Freud is warning us, in other words, that too much repression in an unrealistic society may lead to a sudden outburst of ruthless and destructive behavior. The chief source of this aggressive behavior is a primordial instinct for self-destruction, which Freud called "the death instinct." At the same time, however, human nature is driven by an equally powerful instinct for self-preservation, which Freud called "Eros" (the Greek word for love). The entire phenomenon of life, he declared, can be explained by the concurrent or mutually opposing action of these two instincts.[10] It is Eros, for example, which is responsible for combining men into social units and for devising ways of controlling the death instinct. The most effective means of control is to bring that instinct into the service of Eros by diverting it against the external world. This is the source of man's socially aggressive behavior. The individual directs his aggression against the world instead of against himself. But there are different ways of accomplishing this goal, and the trick is to devise ways that will satisfy the drive without destroying the world. Hence the need for creative and socially acceptable modes of expressing aggression. And for Freud, no better way of meeting these demands had yet been devised than the social system of capitalism.

When Freud first began to reflect upon the implications of the death instinct, he conceived of it as separate from Eros. As his thought matured, however, he moved closer to the notion that they were really the same—distinct perhaps, but not separate. The human reality, in other words, is characterized by a fundamental ambivalence. Neither Eros nor the destructive derivatives of the death instinct can exist independently of each other. As Freud himself puts it, "Libido has a share in every instinctual manifestation." [11] Brought to its logical conclusion, Freud's insight leads to the astonishing claim that every act of violence is implicitly an act of love, while every act of love is implicitly an act of violence.

> It seems as though an instinct of the one sort can scarcely operate in isolation; it is always accompanied—or, as we say, alloyed—with an element from the other side, which modifies its aim or is, in some case, what enables it to achieve that aim. Thus, for instance the instinct of self-preservation is certainly of an erotic kind, but it must nevertheless have aggressiveness at its disposal if it is to fulfill its purpose. So too, the instinct of love, when it is directed towards an object, stands in need of some contribution from the instinct of mastery if it is in any way to possess that object.[12]

Implicit in Freud's thought, then, is the doctrine that man's nature is essentially demonic. Man seeks at one and the same time both to be and not to be. And this means that every human act, because it expresses the whole of man's nature, must be regarded as both creative and destructive.

This fundamental ambivalence, which lies at the center of

human nature, is a fact of the utmost importance. From this concept of human nature Freud concluded that the only healthy societies are those that succeed in substituting creatively aggressive (or socially acceptable) activities for man's natural but highly irrational aggressiveness. Such a society would be founded on a scientific understanding of human nature as it really is, and would bring the death instinct into the service of Eros. In such a society, where *Id* once was there would *Ego* be. But in a society that does not provide creative opportunities for the expression of aggression, the instinct will be forced to choose other means of doing so, such as war, crime, and other acts of barbarism. Many of these acts, including a great deal of crime itself, will of course be represented as essentially rational and legitimate modes of behavior. Barbarism thus becomes institutionalized through self-deception, and society becomes corrupt and pathological. For to institutionalize barbarism in this way is paranoiac. There is nothing more dangerous to the health of a society than to build devious routes to the unconscious and pretend that evil is really a form of virtue. A society that counterfeits evil by institutionalizing it is indeed a very sick society.

The point about all of this is that the barbarism unleashed by the devious expression of aggression is essentially pathological. The degree of pathology is usually proportionate to the degree of self-deception involved. The pathological expression of aggression toward others is sadism, and the more this sadism is counterfeited by pretending it is something else, the more sadistic it becomes. But the most frightening notion of all is Freud's claim that repressed aggression increases the urge for self-destruction.[13] If one thinks out the implications of this doctrine, one realizes that sadistic behavior directed against others, because it is pathologically induced and hence guilt-ridden, rather than displacing the urge for self-destruction will necessarily increase it. In normal circumstances aggression is directed by self-interest primarily against others. In pathological circumstances, however, aggression is directed against the self. Egoism is thus converted into nihilism, the ultimate fate of a corrupt society rooted in self-deception. Nihilism is the pathological incarnation of man's demonic nature induced by the repression of the demonic in the name of the false idols of rational humanism. By ignoring the demonic we inadvertently contribute to its corruption and force it to seek expression in essentially destructive ways. In an age in which the death of mankind may become something more than a literary fantasy, humanity can no longer afford the luxury of ignoring its obligation to face up to the questions I have been asking: Who is Man? How can we know him? What kind of society is fit for him?

Freud defends the free-enterprise competitive system which lies at the basis of capitalism in the light of a theory of human nature which recognizes that man is basically irrational. But the very same view of man has led others to support alternative theories of social control. Many have argued that the dynamics of the open society of capitalism are inconsistent with the needs of most men for security, stability, and authority: needs rooted in the depths of man's nature. And so man naturally resists the challenges of freedom and the open society. This innate fear of freedom, as Erich Fromm points out in his book *Escape from Freedom*, often expresses itself in the desperate craving for security that is most perfectly satisfied by the totalitarian state—the ultimate choice of those whose need to escape from freedom has driven them to the edge of anxiety.[14] B. F. Skinner also admits to this tendency in men to escape from freedom, although for Skinner this urge is an acquired or learned phenomenon, an inevitable consequence of democracy. In the Utopian novel *Walden II*, Professor Burris, who represents the cool voice of behavioral science, cites the existence of this disposition to escape from freedom as a justification for dispensing with democracy and establishing a rigid system of social control. "Most people," says Burris, "live from day to day. They look forward to having children, to seeing the children grow up, and so on. The majority of people don't want to plan. They want to be free of the responsibility of planning. What they ask is merely some assurance that they will be decently provided for. The rest is a day-to-day enjoyment of life. That's the explanation of your Father Divines: people naturally flock to anyone they can trust for the necessities of life." [15]

The open society and the scientific outlook force men into freedom. But, because the fear of freedom is greater than the desire for it, men have engineered exotic avenues of retreat to escape the dreadful demands of that freedom. How else do we explain such phenomena as the appearance in the third century B.C. of pseudo-scientific literature, mostly pseudonymous, and claiming often to be based on divine revelation, which took the ancient superstitions of the East and the more recent fantasies of the Hellenistic masses, dressed them in trappings borrowed from Greek science or Greek philosophy, and won for them acceptance of a large part of the educated class? In later years, scientific theories of the world would be challenged by the much more popular pseudo-scientific approaches of astrology and the teleological theory of occult forces. Other symptoms are the softening of philosophical speculation into quasi-religious dogma which provides the individual with an unchanging rule of life, the appearance of false prophets and oracles, the growth of specialism, and the pathetic reverence for the written word— a readiness to accept statements because they are laid down in books by experts, or even because they are said to be in books. All of these expressions, of what I have earlier called the propaganda of irrationalism, are mechanisms through which men can submit to an unconscious need to escape from freedom. Far better the rigid determinism of astrological fate than the terrifying burden of daily responsibility. And better the security of totalitarianism than the uncertainty of democracy.[16]

But if men wish to surrender their freedom for security,

what is to prevent them from being taken advantage of by the unscrupulous and mercenary? Would it not be wiser, in order to prevent a totalitarianism of the irrational, to place the freedom of men at the disposal of a benevolent and enlightened dictatorship of reason and science? As Skinner himself has put it, we are all controlled by the world in which we live, and part of that world has been and will be constructed by men. We are controlled by such irrational forces as the laws of a market economy based on a profit motive, by desires to satisfy acquired drives for success, status, and power through ruthlessly competitive activities—not to speak of the forces which by accident result from these patterns of behavior. Skinner's question then is this: Are we to continue in this way to be controlled by accident, by tyrants, or by ourselves in effective social design? [17] And his answer recommends placing power in the hands of competent and humane social scientists. This, in his opinion, is the only way to avoid the emotional mystique of "magicalism" and the totalitarianism of power which are the inevitable consequences of democracy.

2. THE GRAND INQUISITOR AND THE "THEOLOGY" OF POWER

One of the classic discussions of this whole issue is Dostoevsky's magnificent story of *The Grand Inquisitor*.[18] The story is set in the fifteenth century in Seville on the eve of an *auto-da-fé*, an occasion on which heretics are burned at the stake so that piety and virtue are once more secured against the influences of free thinking. The next day a stranger appears among the crowd in the marketplace, and though his coming is unobserved, he is instantly recognized. A healing virtue comes from the very touch of his garments. At the steps of the cathedral he raises to life a child who is being brought to burial. In the confusion that follows, the Inquisitor passes by—an old man, tall and erect, with a withered face and sunken eyes, in which there is yet a gleam of light. He orders the arrest of the stranger and at midnight visits him in prison. He asks why he has come to hinder the work of the Church. The stranger replies that he had once promised men unlimited freedom. But the Church, says the Inquisitor, in the name of happiness has been forced to relieve mankind of that intolerable burden. That freedom, the Inquisitor explains, is inconsistent with the nature of man. The stranger listens and seems to understand. When the Inquisitor has finished, the stranger sits for a moment in silence and then suddenly goes up to the old man and kisses him. The Inquisitor opens the prison door upon the dark streets, telling the stranger to go and never to come again. Afterwards, the memory of that kiss glows in the old man's heart, but he holds to his conviction.

The story of the Grand Inquisitor is the classic confrontation between the skeptic who seeks to save men from themselves and the naive humanist who offers men perfect freedom. The Inquisitor is a skeptic who transcends his own skepticism by using his power to control the destiny of the rest of mankind whom he cannot trust to look after themselves. Christ, the naive humanist, has offered men perfect freedom. And mankind has indeed made a heroic effort to achieve that freedom. But the life of freedom is inconsistent with the true nature of man, and so the Church, in the name of humanity, and in order to save mankind from self-destruction, relieved men of the intolerable burden of that freedom. And, says the Inquisitor, this was accomplished by nothing more than giving to men the very thing which Christ denied when he resisted the three temptations. For in those temptations were foreshadowed the whole subsequent history of mankind. They and they alone define the human condition as it really is, and only in a society which is prepared to represent these temptations as virtues can men be expected to survive the wrath of their repressed irrational natures.

The first temptation, materialism, is the cornerstone of the human condition. Remember the first message which Christ rejects: "Thou wouldst go into the world, and art going with empty hands with some promise of freedom which men in their simplicity and their natural unruliness cannot even understand, which they fear and dread—for nothing has ever been more insupportable for a man and a human society than freedom. But seest thou these stones in this parched and barren wilderness? Turn them into bread, and mankind will run after thee like a flock of sheep, grateful and obedient, though forever trembling, lest Thou withdraw Thy hand and deny them Thy bread." But Christ, the humanist and redeemer of man, did not understand the meaning of this message, and he replied that "man does not live by bread alone," thereby sowing the seeds of His own destruction. Little did He realize that in the days to come the spirit of the earth would rise up against Him, led by a new Prometheus proclaiming to the masses that there is no crime and therefore no sin; there is only hunger. Feed men first, then ask of them virtue. That is the message of the temptation which Christ rejected and which would come back to haunt Him throughout the pages of history. For with this motto written on their banners men have risen against and destroyed the temple of Christ, and in its place they have begun to rebuild the terrible tower of Babel. And so, the Inquisitor explains, the Church, in order to avoid the consequences of this reversal of order, and out of genuine love for the many, has offered to endure that freedom which the people have found so dreadful and have traded for security. The Church offers men a society based on miracle, mystery, and authority. And men rejoiced that they were once again led like sheep, and that the terrible gift that had brought them such suffering was at last lifted from their hearts.

The rejection of the first temptation contains another message of existential significance. In rejecting "bread," Christ destroyed the possibility of satisfying the universal and everlasting craving of humanity for security—a craving which can be satisfied not only by bread but by finding someone to worship, namely, he who offers the bread. The object of this worship must be beyond dispute, so that men may worship together in community. Hence the need and urge to conform. This craving for community of worship is the chief misery of every man individually, and of all humanity from the beginning of time. For the sake of this common worship—call it nationalism, or patriotism, or whatever you like—men have slain each other. They have set up gods and challenged one another, crying, "Put away your gods and come and worship ours, or we will kill you and your gods." This, the Inquisitor confesses, is the secret of human nature.

So, the Inquisitor continues, the action of the Church, more than the promises of Christ, is in accord with the true nature of man. For men are weak, vicious, worthless, and rebellious. To promise such a race the bread of heaven is unrealistic; in the eyes of the weak, sinful, and ignoble race of man, the bread of heaven can never compare with the earthly bread of security, profit, and injustice.[19] Indeed, the Inquisitor confesses, so deep is our acknowledgment of man's feebleness that we have permitted him to sin with our sanction; and at times it is even in the name of the Lord that he has been permitted this indulgence. That deception, says the Inquisitor, is our suffering; for we have been forced to lie in the name of a greater good. For the sake of order and obedience to God we have been forced to counterfeit virtue.

Of course, the Inquisitor admits, there will always be a few who will follow the bread of heaven. But what is to become of the tens of millions of creatures who have not the strength to forgo the earthly bread for the sake of the heavenly? Or do Christians and humanists care only for the few at the expense of the numerous weak? Humanistic Christianity might save the few, but it will condemn the many to eternal hell.

In the second temptation, the removal of conscience, Christ was given a further insight into the nature of man. Man is tormented by no greater anxiety than to find someone quickly to whom he can hand over the gift of freedom with which he is born. This freedom can be bought by anyone who is willing to appease man's conscience. Christ, however, would force man to live with his conscience. Now, a man must have something to live for, but instead of providing that meaning for him in the form of miracle, mystery, and dogma, Christ asked man to find it for himself. He would force man against his nature to choose in the knowledge of good and evil. In place of authority and certainty, Christ offered freedom of choice and personal responsibility. But men have found and will continue to find this responsibility a burden too painful to bear, and in the anguish of their suffering they will escape in the only way possible: by denying the message of Christ and declaring that the Truth is not in Him.

The Inquisitor has made a point of deep psychological significance. He is saying that the masses of the people will find their actual experience of freedom to be inconsistent with their expectations; for Christ, like all humanists, made the mistake of promising men that freedom would give them perfect happiness. This deception was necessary if men were to be converted to Christianity in the first place. But freedom is not a means to happiness. It is an end in itself whose possession can bring only anguish and despair. The dissonance produced by this conflict between expectation and reality is the source of much unbearable anxiety. One way of resolving this anxiety is to change our attitude toward the ideology that is the source of our expectations. Rather than blaming ourselves for failing to live up to the challenge of freedom, it is much easier to blame the object of our frustration: the very idea of freedom itself and its embodiment in the institutions of democracy. By rejecting the idea of freedom, which is now regarded as an expression of evil, and substituting for it, in the name of an ultimate truth, the idea of totalitarianism, we succeed both in escaping from anxiety and in escaping from freedom. And so the Inquisitor, in competition with behaviorists like B. F. Skinner, wants men to give their freedom to the Church, because if they do not they will give it away anyhow—perhaps to a less benign, more savage institution.

The Inquisitor has said that there are three powers necessary to conquer and hold captive the conscience of men—miracle, mystery, and authority—and it is not in the nature of man to live without them. If a society does not allow men access to these powers, then they will be driven to satisfy their needs by creating new miracles and myths and worshiping new deeds of sorcery and witchcraft. To expect them to live without these opiates is to expect too much from them. If Christ had really loved man, He would have asked less and would have made his burden lighter.

Finally, the Inquisitor comes to the third temptation, the promise of the unity of mankind in the form of a universal state, to be achieved, if necessary, by means of the sword. Mankind has always striven to organize a universal state. But Christ rejected the sword of Caesar, declaring that the kingdom of heaven and the kingdom of earth were separate. Had He accepted this last council of the mighty spirit, He would have accomplished all that man seeks on earth: that is, someone to worship, someone to keep his conscience, and some means of uniting all in one unanimous and harmonious ant heap. And so, once again, out of a genuine love of mankind, the Church found it necessary to correct the teachings of Christ. "We have taken up the sword," the Inquisitor declares, "and proclaimed ourselves sole rulers of the earth, and when we have triumphed, and the world is united under one sword, we shall plan the universal happiness of man."

But, the Inquisitor intones, in a prophecy of ominous proportions, the final salvation of man shall not be won cheaply. History will bear witness to the price men must pay for the freedom that was falsely purchased. The dream of freedom will end in a nightmare of nihilism and cannibalism. And having consumed its passions in an orgy of self-destruction, the beast (which the false promise of freedom has released) will crawl back to us and lick our feet and splatter them with tears of blood. And we shall sit upon the beast and raise the cup, and on it will be written "mystery." Then and only then will the reign of peace and happiness come to mankind.

The Grand Inquisitor is a profound commentary on the nature of man. In this story we are exposed to the possible consequences of man's vain attempt to live in a state of perfect freedom. Men would rather be happy than free; and happiness depends upon security. The Inquisitor's exhortation exposes, among other things, the consequences of what is perhaps the most serious threat to the human craving for security, namely, the destruction of order, the introduction of innovation into the dogmatic routine of ritual replication. Men cannot tolerate any threat to the continuity of life. Without routines for guidance, life becomes an empty vessel. But the Inquisitor's conviction is tempered by a profound sadness. If the Inquisitor is a realist, he is at least a compassionate one—like the inquisitors who challenged Galileo when he threatened to upset the balance of the eternal order of things.

One of the most compelling and understanding representations of this conflict, between freedom and compassion for man's inability to bear the consequences of that freedom, is Bertolt Brecht's play *The Life of Galileo*. About midway through the play, after Galileo has been officially condemned by the Church and his teachings outlawed from the realm of thought, a young monk and student of mathematics comes to Galileo to confess that he has decided to abandon the study of science for the security of faith. He has made this decision only after many sleepless nights, during which time he attempted to reconcile the papal decree with his own knowledge of science. But finally, the young monk declares, he "succeeded in fathoming the wisdom of that decree" which revealed to him "the danger to mankind that lurks in too much uncontrolled research" (or, to put it another way, in too much freedom). The considerations that led the monk to this conclusion are described as follows:

I grew up as a son of peasants in the Campagna. They were simple people. They knew all about olive-trees, but very little else. While observing the phases of Venus, I can see my parents, sitting by the hearth with my sister, eating their cheese. I see above them the beams blackened by centuries of smoke, and I see clearly their old, work-worn hands and the little spoons they hold. They are not rich, but even in their misfortune there lies concealed a certain invisible order of things. There are those various rounds of duties, from scrubbing the floor, through the seasons in the olive grove, to the payment of taxes. There is even regularity in the disasters that befall them. My father's back becomes bent, not suddenly, but more and more each spring among the olive-trees, just as the child-bearings which have made my mother less and less a woman have followed one another at regular intervals. But they call up the strength to sweat up the stony paths with their baskets, to bear children, yes, even to eat, from the feeling of continuity and necessity which is given them by the sight of the soil, of the trees springing with new green foliage every year, of the little church, and by listening every Sunday to the Bible texts. They have been assured that the eye of God rests upon them; searchingly, yes, almost anxiously—that the whole universe has been built up round them in order that they, the actors, can play their greater or lesser parts. What would my people say if they learned from me that they were really on a little bit of rock that ceaselessly revolves in empty space round another star, one among very many, a comparatively unimportant one? Why is such patience, such acceptance of their misery, either necessary or good today? Why is there still virtue in Holy Writ, which explains everything and has established the necessity of toil, endurance, hunger, resignation, and which now is found to be full of errors? No, I see their eyes grow frightened! I see them dropping their spoons on the hearthstone, I see how they feel cheated and betrayed. So there is no eye resting upon us, they say. We must look after ourselves, untaught, old and worn out as we are? No one has provided a part for us on this earthly, miserable, tiny star which is not independent and round which nothing revolves? There is no meaning in our misery, hunger is simply not-

having-eaten, and not a test of strength; exertion is just stoop-
ing and tugging—with nothing to show. So do you understand
that in that decree of the Holy Congregation I perceive true
maternal compassion, great goodness of soul? [20]

To this insight Dostoevsky's Inquisitor adds that without the
security of routine and without the opportunity to satisfy his
irrational craving for miracle, mystery, and authority, man
will resort to violent and destructive means of self-expression.

And so the Grand Inquisitor takes his place beside Freud
and the other critics of naive humanism. His solution to the
problem differs from those of the other critics, but he shares
in common the same basic fear, which is, in effect, that unless
men stop pretending they are angels in search of perfect freedom, and submit themselves to a system of control that
allows for the expression of their irrational cravings, for mystery, miracle, authority, and security, the result will be the
nightmare of George Orwell's *1984*, haunted by the new
Prometheus who comes to relieve men of the anxiety that
naive humanism has fostered in the deep places of their soul.
After trying to live like angels, men will welcome the opportunity to revert to the state of nature. As Callicles said in his
prophecy: "The reign of humanism and mediocrity will not
last forever. There will come a day when the individual will
achieve his revenge against the society of humanists; there
shall arise men sufficiently endowed by nature to shake off
and break through and escape the chains of mediocrity and
the deception of humanism—men who will tread underfoot
our texts and our spells, our incantations and unnatural laws
and by an act of revolt reveal themselves to be masters instead of slaves." What is more, as Julius Vander (the hero of
The Professor) reminds us, the masses of the people will like
what their new leaders offer them. They are sick and tired
of pretending to be virtuous; in one moment all their enforced
complacency will turn to the vast relief of the practical enjoyment of hatred. The boot stamping on a human face
forever.

3. THE PROMETHEUS OF ROMANTIC INDIVIDUALISM AND THE ESCHATOLOGY OF EVIL

These are not empty prophecies. The New Prometheus, come to liberate man's irrational cravings, is no mere literary fantasy. The world has already experienced at least one such pornographic exercise of power. In Germany during the 1920's and 1930's, Callicles' prophecy was finally fulfilled. The Prometheus of romantic individualism appears in the person of Adolf Hitler addressing a cheering, hysterical multitude voicing their approval of what he tells them.

> It is evident that the stronger has the right before God and the world to enforce his will. History shows us that right as such does not mean a thing unless it is backed up by great power. If one does not have the power to enforce his right, that right alone will profit him absolutely nothing. The stronger have always been victorious. The whole of nature is a continuous struggle between strength and weakness, and eternal victory of the strong over the weak.[21]

Like Callicles, Julius Vander, and O'Brien, the literary expressions of the propaganda of irrationalism which I have discussed, Hitler too launched a popular attack on the *Weltanschauung*, or world-view, of rational humanism.

> Unfortunately, the contemporary world stresses internationalism instead of the innate values of race, democracy and the majority instead of the worth of the great leader. Instead of everlasting struggle the world preaches cowardly pacifism and everlasting peace. These things are the causes of the downfall of all humanity.[22]

> . . . there is no humanitarianism but only an eternal struggle, a struggle which is the prerequisite for the development of all humanity.

> The borderline between man and animals is established by man himself. We see before us the Aryan race which is manifestly the bearer of all culture.[23]

A *Weltanschauung* that denies the idea of struggle is contrary to nature and will breed a people that is guided by it to destruction.[24]

Man has become great through struggle. The first fundamental of any rational *Weltanschaaung* is the fact that on earth and in the universe force alone is decisive. Whatever goal man has reached is due to his originality plus his brutality.[25]

From all this, Hitler drew the most brutal conclusion of all: in Munich, on March 15, 1929, he unleashed the passion that was to lead to conditions under which O'Brien's image of the boot stamping on a human face forever would finally become a concrete reality:

If men wish to live, then they are forced to kill others. The entire struggle for survival is a conquest of the means of existence which in turn results in the elimination of others from the same sources of subsistence. [WILD AND HYSTERICAL CHEERING] [26]

But the spirit of barbarism masquerading as a new promise of freedom did not perish in the ashes of the Third Reich. As audiences in Germany were thrilled by the antihumanistic polemics of Adolf Hitler, so today audiences throughout America are thrilled and inspired by the wild ravings of racists and anti-integrationists. Perhaps you were present when words such as these were spoken:

Of the many forms in which pseudo-humanitarianism attempts to deceive us, the latest is the argument you hear more and more nowadays about the difference between an individual and his race. We are told that we must think only about the individual as an individual, never about his race—that a human being is a human being, and that ends the matter. . . . But you can say with a clear conscience to every integrationist you meet: "You shall not pervert the word 'humanity' to cloak your effort to corrupt our civilization. You shall not masquerade under the banner of Christianity while you sap our strength at the roots and steal our birthright." . . . After you have met Mr. Big Bluff and survived the serpent of evasion, after you have passed through the slough of pseudo-humanitarianism and bogus religion, after you have stripped the mask off the face of political motivation, you will come at long last to the gate of reversal. . . . Let's be clear about it. You are not fighting just for the civilization of the South nor just for the protection of your children. This integration issue is the perfect ground for a greater battle. Here is the place not only to fight integration but to fight the ideology that spawned integration, the ideology of the far left, the overdrift beyond the pivot point, the leeching that would bleed us more and more. This time the sleeping, bemused North must be roused by the South. As I said earlier, these hard-core leftists, striking at you, have betrayed themselves at last. You'll never have a better chance to beat them than you have right here, to save your own society and to save the American way of life for us all. . . . I would urge you to put aside appeasement and defeatism and local politics and economic fears. More depends on your steadfastness than you may realize. Never forget how crucial this battle really is. Our forefathers, down the years, whose faith and valor gave us all we've got, knew how to act in a crisis. They were not easily discouraged. They despised appeasement. So I'm not ashamed to leave you with some lines from an English poet whom our cousins loved when they manned the battlements:

> For all we have and are,
> For all our children's sake,
> Stand up and take the war.
> The foe is at the gate! [27]

Thus speaks Carlton Putnam, leader and spokesman for American racists, in an address to the fifth annual General Conference for District Attorneys, State of Louisiana, held in 1962 in New Orleans. Again I am reminded of the poem by Yeats, and especially of the last two lines.

> And what rough beast, its hour come round at last,
> Slouches towards Bethlehem to be born?

Faced with such possibilities, to be expected whenever the

nature of man is violated by an excessively rationalized humanism, realists like the Grand Inquisitor and B. F. Skinner have argued that the only solution to the paradox of the human condition is to bring mankind under a benevolent dictatorship which will satisfy his need for security and authority while preserving the illusion of freedom; while Freud, on the other hand, favors a more open society which controls aggression by sublimating it into productive and creative activities.

Looked at in this way, the institution of a scientifically ordered system of social control, whether of the Skinnerian or Freudian variety, or else the institution of a religion of authority, as favored by the Grand Inquisitor, does indeed seem far preferable to the risk of annihilation through the pornographic pursuit of evil. But in fact these are not our only options. It is almost certain that by pretending to be angels we shall surely become devils. At the same time, however, no real victory is achieved by so arranging conditions that men are no longer permitted to pursue evil. Denying to men both the right and the opportunity to be evil is as much a negation of their humanity as pretending they are thoroughly virtuous. The possibility of real virtue exists only for a man who has the freedom to choose evil. It is only for the man who has first "lived through" (imaginatively or otherwise) the choice of evil that the real meaning of virtue is disclosed for the first time. But the first stage in the dialectic of human redemption through the imaginative encounter with evil is learning to refuse all illusions: whether it be the illusion of man as an angel led astray by wicked forces from afar, or the illusion of man wholly driven by demonic forces from within. Man exists at the center of a contradiction which can be resolved only by "living through," in imagination and understanding, *all* of his intrinsic possibilities. It is only, to repeat, through the imaginative transcendence of evil that the future of mankind can be secured.

CHAPTER FIVE. HUMANIZATION AND THE EXPERIENCING OF MEANING

The producers and the consumers of spiritual wealth are out of touch! The bridge between them is broken and only a daring spirit here and there can leap the gulf. . . . This coexistence of overproduction on the one side with unsatisfied demand on the other [is] *. . . the special problem of modern life.*
R. G. Collingwood

The world is suffering from a lack of faith in a transcendental truth.
Renouvier

From almost the beginning of man's intellectual history, philosophers have been concerned with the question, How does one create the good society and avoid disorder? As Bruno Bettelheim puts it, in *The Informed Heart*, do we concentrate exclusively on radical reforms within society itself in order to create conditions under which individuals can achieve full realization? Or is this the wrong approach, and would we not be better advised to concentrate on those techniques by means of which individuals can achieve full personal integration and liberation? If we opt for the former, then we lend support to a full-scale program of social reform leading ultimately to a policy of social control. But if, on the other hand, we favor the latter approach, we ought to forget about any social or economic revolutions and concentrate instead on techniques for achieving self-understanding—the hope being that once the majority of men have been liberated from the bondage of their emotions, they would almost automatically create the good society for themselves and for all others.[1]

This conflict has been with us for a long time. In Plato's day it expressed itself as a conflict between politics and education. During the Renaissance it was embodied in the conflict between dogmatic religion, which represented the spirit of security, and science, which represented the spirit of open and free enquiry. More recently, during the 1930's, for example, many found themselves choosing between Marxism and psychoanalysis; while today the problem presents itself in the tension that exists between those who favor scientifically based programs of social control and those, like the existential philosophers, who emphasize the importance of being an individual, and having the courage and wisdom to act as an individual.[2]

I have already pointed out that theories of social control derive much of their appeal from the realistic appraisal of man as a being who fears freedom more than he desires it, and who will, if left to himself, surrender that freedom to whomever is clever enough to take advantage of the circumstances. Since men will inevitably surrender their freedom, Utopian-minded social scientists, like B. F. Skinner, would rather see them surrender it to competent and reliable social scientists than to sophists and opportunists who would lead the human race to ruin through the pornographic pursuit of power; while, for what are basically the same reasons, skeptics like the Grand Inquisitor recommend the sacraments of mystery, miracle, and authority, as embodied in the Church, if mankind is to be saved. In the remaining chapters, I propose to discuss some alternative theories of social control.

1. PLATO: A HUMANIST THEORY OF SOCIAL CONTROL

Most of the issues faced by the contemporary philosopher who worries about the individual in society have already been discussed by Plato. Like the critics of our own time, Plato was confronted by the slow but steady growth of the propaganda of irrationalism. The society in which he lived had been corrupted by the pornographic pursuit of power, made all the more corrupt by those intellectual pimps for power, the Sophists, who perverted the integrity of reason by forcing it into the service of expediency, who specialized in manufacturing arguments which sought to represent evil as a necessary means to a greater good, and who were only too happy to lie in behalf of a cause which they knew to be unjust. These are the "clerks" whom Julien Benda accuses of betraying the trust of mankind.

Plato believed that the chief source of disorder in his own society was the hypocrisy of those who pretended to be virtuous, on the one hand, while all the time behaving contrary to their explicit beliefs. In such a society young people will grow up with ideological expectations which are inevitably disappointed by their actual experiences. The result of this discrepancy is an anxiety which is resolved either by excessive conformism or by rebelliousness. Either way, happiness becomes virtually impossible. And so, says Plato, "to produce a different type of character, educated on standards different from those of public opinion, is impossible; to escape harm and grow up on right lines in our present society is something that can fairly be called miraculous." [3]

Plato's account of the education of a typical middle-class Athenian youth is well worth attending to and ought to remind us of what goes on in our own society.[4] He begins by drawing attention to the behavior of parents who tell their children to be just and virtuous but by their own actions make it clear that what they really value about justice is the social prestige it brings, rather than anything intrinsic to the idea of justice itself. In this regard, the priests do little to promote a more genuine reverence for virtue when they preach against sin but let it be known that evil is redeemable through sacrifice and charitable donations—while just for good measure the poets tell us (with the support of the priests) that the just man will be remembered for posterity and in the next world his life will be one of continued festivity, as if the supreme reward of virtue was to be drunk for all eternity. The message that comes through the medium of such behavior is that whether or not you are really just is not nearly as important as whether you have the right image. Having the right image is by itself sufficient to secure for you the power, family connections, and other things which are procured for the just man by a good reputation. This is well demonstrated by the tendency to show respect and bestow honors upon men of dubious moral character providing they have wealth and power, while virtuous but poor men are ignored and despised.

Plato's complaint was shared by many others, like the playwright Aristophanes, whose play *The Knights* lays bare the absurdity inherent in the ease with which men of weak character are able to succeed in politics. In one scene, in particular, the general Demosthenes is trying to persuade a sausage seller to unseat Cleon, the democratic leader:

SAUSAGE SELLER: Tell me this, how can I, a sausage seller, be a big man like that?

DEMOSTHENES: The easiest thing in the world. You've got all the qualifications: low birth, marketplace training, insolence.

SAUSAGE SELLER: I don't think I deserve it!

DEMOSTHENES: Not deserve it? It looks to me as if you've got too good a conscience. Was your father a gentleman?

SAUSAGE SELLER: By the gods, no! My folks were scoundrels.

DEMOSTHENES: Lucky man! What a good start you've got for public life.

SAUSAGE SELLER: But I can hardly read!

DEMOSTHENES: The only trouble is that you know anything. To be a leader of the people isn't for learned men, or honest men, but for the ignorant and vile. Don't miss this golden opportunity.

Well, says Plato, what do you think is likely to be the effect of this sort of talk and behavior on the minds of young men who have enough natural intelligence to gather the implications of what they hear for their own lives, the sort of person they ought to be, and the sort of ends they ought to pursue? What, for example, will be the result of preaching fidelity, virtue, and justice to your teen-age son at the same time you are cheating on your wife and your friends, and enjoying every minute of it? Such a young man, says Plato, may very well be imagined to say to himself something like this: "Shall I by justice mount the higher, or by deceit, and there dig in for life? For it is clear from what they tell me that if I am just, it will bring me no advantage but only trouble and loss, unless I also have a reputation for justice; whereas if I am unjust, but can contrive to get a reputation for justice, I shall have a marvelous time. Well then, since the sages tell me that appearance counts for more than reality and determines our happiness, I had better think entirely of appearances; I must put up a façade that has all of the outward appearance of virtue, but I must always have at my back the cunning wily fox.

"You may, of course, object that it is not so easy to be wicked and never be found out. But then, nothing worth-while is easy. And in any case, what a challenge to my intelligence and ingenuity. It is certainly not very challenging to be good, is it? Nevertheless, if maintaining the appearance of virtue is what counts, this can easily be accomplished through the formation of various clubs and societies which will engage in charitable and philanthropic activities—and of course we can always learn the art of public speaking and take courses in how to win friends and influence people. In short, the thing to do, if you want to get ahead in this world, is *to sin first and sacrifice afterwards from the proceeds*." [5]

But not all the young men who grow up in this absurd world of hypocrisy become conformists. Some react more violently, turning to the pornographic pursuit of immoralism, like Plato's Callicles, the character from the dialogue *Gorgias*, who encourages the psychopath in us by urging young men to satisfy their irrational appetites to the fullest. Still others will react violently but, unlike Callicles, they will do so in order to bring about a renaissance of virtue, like those who followed the cult of "immoralism" so popular in France during the 1920's. As Simone de Beauvoir says in the first volume of her autobiography:

All around me people deplored falsehood, but were careful to avoid the truth; if I found so much difficulty in speaking freely now, it was because I felt it was repugnant to make use of the counterfeit money that was current in my environment. I lost no time in embracing the principles of immoralism. Of course I did not approve of people stealing out of self-interest or going to bed with someone for the pure pleasure of it; but if these became quite gratuitous acts, acts of desperation and revolt—and, of course, quite imaginary—I was prepared to stomach all the vices, the rapes, and the murders one might care to mention. Doing wrong was the most uncompromising way of repudiating all connections with respectable people.

A refusal to use hollow words, false moralizing and its too-easy consolations: the literature of those days was presenting this negative attitude as a positive ethical system. It was turning our restlessness into a crusade; we were seeking for salvation. If we had renounced our class it was in order to get closer to the Absolute. . . . Immoralism was not just a defiance against society; it was a way of reaching God. . . . The important thing was to use whatever means one could to find release from the world, and then one would come within reach of eternity.[6]

Finally, there are young men like Richard Wishnetsky who, on the morning of February 12, 1966, murdered Rabbi Morris Adler in full view of the congregation of Shaarey Zedek synagogue of Detroit, as a protest against the hypocrisy and phoniness of the world in which he was raised. Before committing his unhappy but prophetic act, Wishnetsky addressed the congregation. His words were recorded by the same tape recorder that had registered Rabbi Adler's Bar Mitzvah sermon moments before.

This congregation is a travesty and an abomination. It has made a mockery by its phoniness and hypocrisy of the beauty and spirit of Judaism. . . . It is composed of men, women, and children who care for nothing except their vain egotistical selves. With this act I protest a humanly horrifying and hence unacceptable situation.[7]

In a note written the day before the fatal event occurred, Richard Wishnetsky left with us a lucid account of his motives and of the significance of what he was about to do:

My distorted, disoriented voice, either barely uttered or tremendously violent, gives you a slight horrifying glimpse into the dehumanized future that awaits you and your unfortunate children, who will be healthy, comfortable, and secure beyond your fondest dreams and just as diseased. Since I feel that I am no longer able to make any significant creative contributions, I shall make a destructive one. What happened in Shaarey Zedek happens only once in a lifetime. . . . Suffer in your frozen hells of apathy, boil in the self-hate of outraged impotence. Listen to my voice, you deaf ones. Listen to how sick, sad, lonely, and forlorn it is.[8]

The tragedy of Richard Wishnetsky was precisely what Plato wanted to avoid. He understood that human happiness depends upon something more than efficiency and being well adjusted. There must be something like an *experience of meaning* if men are to be genuinely happy. The essence of human nature, according to Plato, is complex. It contains a spirited capacity for aggressiveness and irrational behavior. But it also contains a rational capacity to comprehend the structure of Being. It is difficult for us to understand what the Greek philosophers meant by the contemplation of pure Being; but it was not unrelated to the life of constant self-examination which Socrates stressed, and must clearly be distinguished from what could alternatively be called "having an explanation," which explains *how things come about* but does not produce anything like an experience of *meaning*.

This point is very well made by Plato in a famous passage from the *Phaedo*, in which Socrates addresses his friends on the eve of his death. He explains how as a young man he hopefully read through the works of the philosopher Anaxagoras, who promised to explain the behavior of things in terms of their rational causes and who argued that the universe had been ordered by mind.

I decided that if this were true, Mind must do all its ordering in the fashion that is best for each individual thing. Hence, if one wanted to discover the cause for anything coming into being or perishing or existing, the question to ask was how it was best for that thing to exist or to act or be acted upon. On this principle, then, the only thing that a man had to think about, whether in regard to himself or anything else, was what is best, what is the highest good; though of course he would also have to know what is bad, since knowledge of good involves knowledge of bad. Within these reflections I was delighted to think I had found in Anaxagoras an instructor about the cause of things after my own heart. . . . I imagined that in assigning the cause of particular things and of things in general he would proceed to explain what was the individual best and the general good; and I wouldn't have sold my hopes for a fortune. I made all haste to get hold of the books, and read them as soon as ever I could, in order to discover without delay what was best and what was worst.

And then, my friends, from my marvelous height of hope I came hurtling down. For as I went on with my reading I found the man making no use of mind, not crediting it with any causality for setting things in order, but finding causes in things like air and ether and water and a host of other absurdities. It seemed to me that his position was like that of a man who said that all the actions of Socrates are due to his mind, and then attempted to give the causes of my several actions by saying that the reason why I am now sitting here is that my body is composed of bones and sinews, and the bones are hard and separated by joints, while the sinews, which can be tightened or relaxed, envelop the bones along with the flesh and skin which hold them together; so that when the bones move about in their sockets, the sinews, by lessening or increasing the tension, make it possible for me at this moment to bend my limbs, and that is the cause of my sitting here in this bent position. Analogous causes might also be given of my conversing with you, sounds, air currents, streams of hearing, and so on and so forth, to the neglect of the true causes; to wit, that inasmuch as the Athenians have thought it better to condemn me, I too in my turn think it better to sit here, and more right and proper to stay where I am and submit to such punishment as they enjoin. For, by Jingo, I fancy these same sinews and bones would long since have been somewhere in Megara or Boettia, impelled by their notion of what was best, if I had not thought it right and proper to submit to the penalty appointed by the state rather than take to my heels and run away. No: to call things like that causes is quite absurd; it would be true to say that if I did not possess things like that—bones and sinews and so on— I shouldn't be able to do what I had resolved upon; but to say that I do what I do because of them—and that too when I am acting with my mind—and not because of my choice of what is best, would be to use extremely careless language. Fancy not being able to distinguish between the cause of a thing and that without which the cause would not be a cause. It is evidently this latter that most people, groping in the dark, call by the name of cause, a name which doesn't belong to it.[9]

Implicit in Plato's example is a distinction between two questions: *What* is Man? and *Who* is Man? The answer to the first is an *explanation* which sets man in his proper context. His behavior is explained by an appeal to *causes*. But explanations by themselves do not provide the meaning without which there can be no answer to the question, Who is man? For the Greeks, the question, Who is man? meant, What is the *purpose* of human existence? or What are the ideal conditions under which man perfects himself? This is the question to which Plato's *Republic* is addressed. And his answer, while not entirely satisfactory, cannot but impress anyone who comes to understand it as one of the great moments in the history of Western thought.

Plato believed that only the just life was fit for man. A man can be happy only when he is doing what is in accordance with his nature. To this extent Plato is a humanist. But he also believed that just as a man possesses a rational capacity for justice, so he is equally possessed by an irrational capacity for destructive acts. And, unlike the naive humanist, Plato was just enough of a skeptic to doubt whether if left to nature a man would be just rather than unjust. Unless some deliberate effort is made to control the irrational appetites, Plato said, the natural tendency is for men to be unjust, which is a tragedy. It is tragic because to the extent to which a man is possessed by the irrational appetites, he is not doing what he is meant to do. His existence does not coincide with his essence. For this reason, one of the chief purposes of society is to control the irrational.

But just as a man's irrational appetites must be carefully controlled, so his native goodness and rationality must be elicited or drawn out of him by an equally deliberate act of control. Thus Plato has it over the naive humanist by recognizing that whereas a man does not have to be taught to be evil (he comes to this quite naturally), he does have to be taught to be good. Plato therefore devised his ideal republic as a means of both controlling man's basic irrationality while at the same time providing for the maximum expression of his rationality. And his concept of justice is based, therefore, on a rapprochement between reason and unreason. Indeed, he often speaks of the healthy soul as a harmony of competing elements. Or, in more contemporary terms, the healthy soul is one whose various capacities or dispositions are perfectly integrated. The integration of personality is the basis of justice in the individual, and because society is but the outward reflection of the soul, it is the basis of the good society as well. The real concern of justice, writes Plato, is not with external actions but with a man's inward self. The just man will not allow the elements which make up his inward self to trespass on each other's functions or interfere with each other, but, by keeping all in tune, like the notes of a scale, will in the truest sense set his house in order, and be his own lord and master and at peace with himself. When he has bound these elements into a single controlled and orderly whole, and so unified himself, he will be ready for action of *any* kind, whether personal, financial, political, or commercial; and whenever he calls any course of action just and fair, he will mean that it contributes to and helps to maintain this disposition of mind, and will call the knowledge which controls such action wisdom. Similarly, by injustice he will mean any action destructive of this disposition, and will call the mentality which controls such action ignorance.[10]

The point that Plato makes in this masterful and eloquent definition of justice is that any particular act a man does expresses the *whole* of his character. Likewise, the behavior of society in any particular respect tends to reflect the entire character of that society. It is not possible to be weak in one respect but healthy in all others. A society that is corrupt with respect to its military activities, for example, will very likely turn out upon examination to be morally corrupt as well. A society that treats some of its members as inferior to others, which denies justice to certain individuals and over-indulges others, is sick and corrupt in its very essence. And if the individual members of a society are unjust, then no amount of efficiency and control at the level of government, law, and institutional reform can prevent the inevitable destruction of that society. In short, unless the individuals who make up that society have achieved personal integration (so that they are consistently just in all their activities, not only when it is convenient or expedient), whatever superficial justice may appear to characterize that society will soon give way to an explicit display of barbarism and decadence. For this reason, Plato and his followers reject any approach to society that believes that so long as we have the proper institutions, society will work fine. If society is a reflection of human character, which is in turn a product of a systematic attempt to achieve integration, then "education," the technology of psychic integration, must be given precedence over "politics," the technology of social control and social reform.

For Plato, the function of education is partly therapeutic. Education is the process through which a person becomes human. But it is not simply socialization, the technique through which individuals are adjusted to society by incorporating the goals of that society. Education is a discipline of self-mastery, an experience through which each individual comes to terms with the demonic.

Plato has seen something important about the human condition. In the first place, he seems clearly to have anticipated the doctrine already discussed, that men seem by nature unable to bear the burden of the freedom they so desperately crave. They are therefore disposed to adopt a variety of irrational and exotic mechanisms in order to escape the freedom and responsibility that the just life requires. This view presupposes something very much like the Freudian doctrine of psychological ambivalence (as expressed in the primordial tension between *eros* and the death instinct). It is also reminiscent of the metaphysical doctrine of Sartre about the duplicity of human consciousness which seeks both "to-be-what-it-is-not" and "not-to-be-what-it-is." Consciousness, for Sartre, *is* freedom. But the chief activity of consciousness consists in a vain attempt to escape from freedom.

But at this point Plato parts company with the existentialist and sounds much more like Freud. The existentialist, like Sartre, stresses the importance of individual efforts to accept the implications of freedom and of courageously resisting temptations to escape. For Plato, however, the flight from being, or descent into inauthenticity, can be prevented only by direct and positive interference from outside. An individual can never be trusted to educate himself. He must therefore be educated, often against his will, until he learns to take charge of himself. Unlike Sartre, Plato (and Aristotle, too, for that matter) believed that no man in adult life can come to know virtue unless the habit of virtue has already been acquired in early youth. Persons brought up under unfortunate and corrupt circumstances are simply beyond remedy: which, of course, seems to imply the further doctrine that a person who has been poorly brought up cannot be held responsible for his acts; which is precisely the conclusion that many today are drawing from the discovery of the influences of early environment on adult character. But this is not in fact what either Plato or Aristotle had in mind when they stressed the importance of early experiences. While Plato doubts whether moral reform is a real possibility for persons whose characters have already been hardened by years of bad habits, he would nevertheless have agreed with Sartre that nothing, not even an unfavorable early environment, can excuse a man from *responsibility* for his moral weakness. For Plato, however, this means that one is condemned to a self-chosen life of eternal damnation if one has been unlucky. The penalty you pay is the life you lead answering to the pattern you resemble.[11] Whereas for Sartre, there is always the possibility of a sudden conversion, even in adult life: as he himself witnessed during the war when many Frenchmen recovered their humanity and their morality when faced with Nazi bayonets.

For Plato, the control of the environment over the individual has two functions. The first is to repress and sublimate the irrational. The second is to elicit the rational. What separates Plato from the naive humanist is his recognition of the fact that man is not simply corrupted by society, but that the corrupting influences of society have their origin in man himself. But then, says Plato, it is not enough simply to repress the irrational in order to guarantee the good society. We must do more than this and teach men how to exercise their native goodness. Of course, virtue cannot be taught as though it were an ordinary skill, like shipbuilding. But there is a way of eliciting it which is more than a matter of chance. Virtue, in other words, is a special kind of knowledge. The process through which virtue is elicited is twofold. The first stage is governed by the principle of *mimesis* or imitation. Virtue is a habit which becomes reinforced only through constant repetition. In this respect, Plato is a thoroughgoing behaviorist. The child learns to be virtuous by imitating his parents, who are expected to set good examples. Indeed, the whole environment must exemplify virtue, goodness, beauty, harmony, and so on. Only in such an environment can the individual psyche free itself from the bondage of disorder. But where the environment itself fails to exemplify the embodiment of virtue, then one can hardly expect the individual psyche to remain intact.

Let us take an example from our own experience. American culture is suffering from a widespread neurosis. We are currently witnessing an acceleration of crime and violence, as well as a variety of acts of civil disobedience—all of which tend to undermine the traditional concept of the rule of law in favor of a state of moral anarchy. American society, in short, is on the edge of mutiny.

But Plato would say that this is precisely what we should expect in a society that subordinates truth, beauty, and justice to the principles of use and profit; that rapes the natural beauty of the land in the name of progress and surrounds every city with scrap heaps, garbage dumps, and burial grounds for old cars, in total indifference to the needs of the senses for order, beauty, and majesty. Instead of accommodating the need for an experience of beauty, the fouling of the environment, in which we have become so expert, evokes the cruder instincts in man to extend this policy of rape and exploitation upon himself.[12] Our interpersonal relationships are but reflections of what we are forced from childhood to imitate and assimilate from the physical environment in which we live. We have, in effect, created a culture which virtually sabotages our efforts to be human. But we intuitively realize this, with the result that we tend to react with profound disappointment and frustration to what our culture presents us with. The fear of being totally swallowed up by this culture of our own creation becomes, as it were, an acquired drive of powerful force. The individual now becomes driven by his disappointment and fear that he might, deprived of a chance to realize his spiritual potentialities (which he will always at least unconsciously experience within himself), become nonhuman.

In short, a chief source of man's irrationality is his disappointment over the prospect of not being able to realize his own intrinsic potentialities. This experience of disappointment is one of the primary sources of man's destructive behavior, both toward others and toward himself. Its ultimate consequence is the transformation of the human into the nonhuman. This is what drives young men like Agatson (the tragic hero of John Clellon Holmes's novel *Go*) and Richard Wishnetsky wild. And the tragedy is that when good men such as these are driven by their passion for liberty to protest the outrage of social injustice, they invariably resort to mindless acts of violence. The imagination of revolt gives way to the nihilism of mutiny and the apocalyptic madness of heroic individualism.

The essence of this all too human posture is conveyed by Dostoevsky's sensitive portrait of Alyosha Karamazov:

... he was to some extent a youth of our last epoch—that is, honest in nature, desiring truth, seeking for it and believing in it, and seeking to serve it at once with all the strength of his soul, seeking for immediate action, and ready to sacrifice everything, life itself, for it.[13]

Dostoevsky's own critical but compassionate response to the profound emptiness of this wasted heroism speaks for itself.

... these young men unhappily fail to understand that the sacrifice of life is, in many cases, the easiest of all sacrifices, and that to sacrifice, for instance, five or six years of their seething youth to hard and tedious study, if only to multiply tenfold their powers of serving the truth and the cause they have set before them as their goal—such a sacrifice is utterly beyond the strength of many of them.[14]

Needless to say, Plato would never permit the assault on the sensibilities that is bound to disturb any sensitive traveler in America. If the child learns to be virtuous by imitating virtuous models, the environment in which the child lives must be ideal, as must be the conduct and behavior of those individuals with whom he lives. Once the child has successfully internalized the values of society, which become his own personal goals, he will have become conditioned or habituated to virtuous behavior.

But justice is not simply a matter of doing just things, not simply a matter of being habituated to behave in socially acceptable ways. Genuine virtue consists in doing just things *justly*. The habits that in the beginning serve only as means to the realization of certain ends (like avoiding being punished, or being rewarded with parental approval) must eventually become "functionally autonomous," so that they are performed for their own sake. One's habits, in other words, must cease to be mere habits and become choices. Only then can the individual begin to understand the intrinsic rightness of his own actions. And only then can the values implied in such acts become genuine objects of understanding.

The behavior of justice, then, is intentional behavior, behavior by a conscious being who is aware of himself as choosing to do certain things because he sees the point of what he is doing and understands the meaning of his acts. It is this understanding and experience of meaning which, for Plato, is the strongest reinforcing agency in a person's behavior. And because what he does is in keeping with his real nature, his virtue is the source of genuine happiness. Happiness, for Plato, is the experience of the harmony between one's behavior and one's inner nature. Or, to put it another way, *happiness lies in choosing to be yourself, choosing to be what you have been socialized and conditioned to be.* This is what it means for your existence to coincide with your essence.

And so Plato is saying, in effect, that *the aim of education is the production of individuals who want to act as they have to act.* Freedom is the recognition of necessity. But—and this is the all-important point for Plato—the necessity according to which we will and act is an objective necessity which has its origin both in the eternal nature of man and in the transcendental or timeless truth of which man's rational soul is a copy. The very foundation of Plato's philosophy is the principle that the historical world of time and change is but the moving image of eternity. And progress is therefore to be measured by the degree to which the earthly city corresponds with the ideal structure of the eternal city.

But this belief in the existence of an unchanging and timeless transcendental truth which is independent of experience is the chief weakness of Plato's philosophy. The theory that truth is an idea which exists prior to the attempt to realize it and is, if you like, a kind of blueprint to be followed in the construction of the good society, can never be demonstrated. To begin with, if there were such a truth, by what criterion could it possibly be evaluated? As any particular act of judgment is necessarily sensuous and temporal, it is difficult to see how such an act could either be identical with or even resemble a non-sensuous, timeless, or eternal object. Even if such a resemblance were possible, we could only measure it if we possessed a criterion which was neither the temporal act of consciousness, on the one hand, nor the eternal object itself. But such a criterion is impossible to conceive except by identifying it with one or other of the very entities between which it is supposed to mediate in the first place. These logical objections to the idea of a separation between truth and experience seem to me to be impossible to overcome.

There are also a number of psychological objections. For example, what is to prevent one's idea of what constitutes the essence of truth from becoming a self-fulfilling prophecy? But of most importance is the imminent danger that whether or not our beliefs are true, they are nevertheless a source of deep security to us, and because of this we tend to resist every effort to change them and seek every manner of excuse for going on believing as we are accustomed. Nothing, in fact, is more dangerous to human society than the dogma that truth is the sort of thing that can be defined and specified once and for all. This dogma is one of the chief sources of the pathological use of power as a means to protect truth from change.

2. EXISTENTIALISM AND THE SUBJECTIVITY OF TRUTH

In reaction to this notion, the twentieth century has witnessed a swing to the opposite direction, toward the relativistic theory of truth as a mere product of social experience. But relativism, as I have previously argued, is a further source of the pathological use of power. For if each man is the measure of truth, then the only way of settling disputes between conflicting claims is power. The problem today, then, is to reconsider the relation between truth and subjective experience, in such a way as to avoid both the Scylla of dogmatic objectivism, on the one hand, and the Charybdis of radical subjectivism, on the other.

The basis of the rapprochement is contained in Kierkegaard's cryptic remark that truth is subjectivity. By this Kierkegaard did not mean anything so naive as that truth is whatever your subjective feelings tell you it is. The *universality of the subjective*, which is the source of existential objectivity, is not to be confused with the mere *subjectivization of truth*. For Kierkegaard, the doctrine that truth is subjectivity means not that truth is a private creation but rather that the objectivity of truth constitutes itself only within the subjective life of the individual. I do not first learn the truth and then act according to it; I act first and then come to an understanding of the implicit truthfulness of my action. We do not know in order to act, we act in order to know. The concept of mind as a consciousness of truth is replaced by the concept of mind as a truthful consciousness. This leads into the heart of existential philosophy, whose central problem is that of reconciling the objectivity of truth, which has a transcendental origin, with the subjective presence of that truth in experience. If man is a seeker after truth, it is he who is ultimately responsible for creating the conditions under which this truth can be encountered. The source of self-making is not simply, as Plato would have it, *the experience of meaning* but *the experiencing of the creation of meaning*.

Man, in other words, is responsible not only for discovering the truth but for creating the conditions under which this discovery becomes possible. And since the truth that is discovered is not only *my* truth but has a universality valid for all men, in prescribing or legislating a value for myself I at the same time prescribe it for all men: and I assume a responsibility hitherto reserved only for gods. This responsibility is the source both of the nobility and the despair of man. It is the source of nobility because it means that the future is in our own hands and is not just the inevitable outcome of a pre-existing plan. But it is the source of anguish because it means that we must grope toward a future of our own choosing without the aid of external authorities, guided only by our self-chosen commitments and by the intuitive demands of our inner consciousness.

CHAPTER SIX. THE APOCALYPTIC VISION AND THE NIHILISM OF DESPAIR

To adapt the self to the new realities of power is to feel a new kind of dread, to sense a new kind of guilt, to be weighted by a new kind of helplessness quite different from our helplessness before either gods or the natural order.
Wylie Sypher

Whenever man shudders before the menace of his own work and longs to flee from the radically demanding historical hour, there he finds himself near to the apocalyptic vision of a process that cannot be arrested.
Martin Buber

There is no greater danger to an individual than the temptation to give up his freedom for the sake of security. In choosing not to be free, the individual accepts the invitation to anonymity that society constantly extends. "Join with us and submit to our authority and you shall be free" is the message we so often hear. But what is not immediately evident in this attractive and tempting offer is that in accepting it we run the risk of initiating a process that may well lead to total dehumanization. Admittedly, there is no society without authority; but there is an important difference between the *celebration of freedom within the limits of authority* and the *subordination of freedom to authority*. In the first case, the structure of authority is itself grounded in the exercise of freedom. But in the second case, the exercise of freedom becomes utterly dependent upon authority. This dependency is the basis of the authoritarian society.

In the authoritarian society the individual loses his humanity. Interpersonal relationships are transferred from the realm of subjectivity to the realm of objectivity. The relationship between one person and another is mediated by rules. The person is defined in terms of his function and is encouraged to identify completely with his roles. In such a society there is no longer any need for feelings like trust, compassion, and concern. The "risk" of existence, which is the source of an existential void, is now replaced by massive structures which fill in the void and make the world a safer, more secure, and more permanent place to live in.

But without compassion, without the anguish that comes from living in trust, the individual is emptied of all human content. He becomes what T. S. Eliot has so aptly called a "hollow man":

> We are the hollow men
> We are the stuffed men
> Leaning together
> Headpiece filled with straw. Alas!
> Our dried voices, when

We whisper together
Are quiet and meaningless
As wind in dry grass
Or rats' feet over broken glass
In our dry cellar

The hollow man is without feeling and compassion, but not without emotion. The result of dehumanization is not simply a state of passivity. It is worse: a weakening of the ego and, consequently, a loss of the capacity for restraining the instinct for aggression. Writers like Schopenhauer, Nietzsche, and Freud have made us painfully aware of this. As Yeats has put it, in his poem "The Second Coming," "the best lack all conviction, while the worst are full of passionate intensity." Through the ritual of conformism, in which the ceremony of innocence is drowned, the individual is reshaped into a potential psychopath. Driven by guilt for having murdered the God within, he will seek opportunities to displace that guilt through the expression of aggression directed against others. The frustration of being unable to love and to pay homage to the demands of *eros* gives birth to a passionate intensity in the service of the instinct to self-destruction.

We must, therefore, take seriously Freud's claim that the instinct for death is an ineradicable part of the nature of man. This is the reason why our fascination with violence, death, torture, and terror can so easily become pathological, and why our ways of representing these experiences often border on pornography. If we recognize this about ourselves, then we must stop pretending that man's irrationality is merely the result of poor socialization and education. Placing the whole blame on the environment and the social system does not contribute to the deepest possible understanding of the human condition. We must distinguish between *precipitating* and *predisposing* causes. No doubt the stresses of modern society have precipitated a breakdown of human relations. But the predisposing causes, as Sartre has explained, have their origin in the ontological disposition of man "to-be-what-he-is-not" and "not-to-be-what-he-is." [1]

From this ontological fact, we are driven to the realization that every human act is fundamentally ambivalent. The same act through which I reach out to caress you with tenderness is also a potentially aggressive one; indeed, the feeling of aggression is encapsulated within the feeling of love. Whenever a convicted murderer or rapist or criminal is punished, the passion that leads us to punish him is not entirely driven by a commitment to justice. Implicit in the passion for justice is the passion of revenge: the offender must be punished not simply because he broke the law but because he dared to commit that awful indiscretion, to do what we all desire but cannot do. We are all, as Dostoevsky says, underground men, driven by our very nature to "vomit up reason." And so, writes Dostoevsky:

> Out of sheer ingratitude, man will play you a dirty trick just to prove that men are still men and not the keys of a piano. . . . And even if you could prove that a man is only a piano key, he would still do something out of sheer perversity—he would create destruction and chaos just to gain his point. . . . And if this could in turn be analyzed and prevented by predicting that it would occur, then man would deliberately go mad to prove his point.[2]

But just as there is no pure act of love or virtue, so there is no pure act of evil. The murderer in the very act of murder may release a hidden capacity for compassion which has hitherto been blocked by years of pretending to be either wholly good or wholly bad, depending on which role has been assigned to him.

The duplicity of man's being is the starting point of the existential philosopher's attempt to answer the question, Who is Man? As Sartre says, man is freedom. Yet he seeks to escape from freedom through deliberate acts of bad faith. By bad faith Sartre means the tendency to deceive oneself into believing that one possesses a truth which is in reality a falsehood, and which one *knows* to be a falsehood. Or, conversely, it is the tendency to conceal from oneself a truth which one knows. Indeed, it is only because consciousness knows the truth in the first place that it can be so clever about concealing or distorting it. Sartre says, "I must know the truth very exactly *in order to* conceal it more carefully" [3]

1. THE PASSION OF RACISM

There are many avenues of bad faith, and we are all pursuing them whether we know it or not. One of the most effective avenues of escape is prejudice, and especially race prejudice, or "racism." Racism, the belief in the biological and cultural inferiority of certain human groups with respect to other groups, is indigenous to the very origins of our society. Long before the appearance of the Negro, the exploration and occupation of territories occupied by the North American Indian was justified by the conviction that the Indian was a savage, less human and less developed than the European. As Susan Sontag says, rather bluntly:

> America was founded on a genocide, on the unquestioned assumption of the right of white Europeans to exterminate a resident, technologically backward colored population in order to take over the continent.[4]

This belief, combined with the idea of progress, which had for centuries been the underlying ideology of Western culture, magically transformed the genocidal occupation and destruction of the Indian into the fulfillment of a messianic destiny: just as today the ruthless slaughter of large numbers of Vietnamese has been magically transformed into a fight for justice against the dark forces of communism. This too is commonly regarded as a necessary expedient, necessary for the preservation of freedom throughout the world.

But racism, like the ideology of progress, is a passion which rationalizes aggression by concealing the aggressive impulse under the cover of a rational purpose. The behavior engaged in is not just immoral; it amounts virtually to a pornographic celebration in bestiality. And it is for this reason that racism will not yield to argument; it is thoroughly immune to all forms of reason. Racism is not an exercise of reason but an expression of the propaganda of irrationalism. It is not, therefore, a result of a mistake in reasoning. A man does not become a racist because he has misinterpreted the evidence; he misinterprets the evidence because he is already a racist. Being a racist has little or nothing to do with how one is affected by scientific evidence. It is rather a passion chosen in order to satisfy needs which would otherwise have found equally irrational outlets. Racism is an apocalyptic phenomenon which proceeds from the exhausted imagination of a defeated culture, a culture that has lost faith in its basic values.

Racism is a passion which provides a source of security for the individual who embraces it by releasing him from the anguish of being human. One is normally disposed to treat racism as a learned response to certain specifiable stimuli, or as a function of environmental conditioning. But I am concerned more with the morality and ontology of racism regarded as a mode of *being-in-the-world*, a way of life which is chosen for reasons independent of its causes. Hence, to *explain* racism as a learned attitude does not contribute to an *understanding* of it as a significant human phenomenon, as a way of being. The causal analysis of racism must be supplemented by a "phenomenological" analysis if we are fully to comprehend its significance. A phenomenology of racism neither invalidates nor constitutes an alternative to a causal or functional analysis. Each is addressed to a distinct question. A science of racism answers the questions, What are the causes of racism? How is the attitude acquired and modified? A phenomenological analysis inquires into the ontology and human significance of racism. It answers the question, What is the significance of racism as a human way of being-in-the-world? The sciences of racism (sociology and psychology) present racism as an acquired habit which functions psychologically as an attitude that orders experience and sociologically as an institution that orders society. Racism also has economic and political significance. A phenomenology of racism, however, reveals its structure as a "lived-experience," as an intentional way of negating the humanity of another *in order to* negate one's own humanity, as a flight from freedom and responsibility; or, as Sartre puts it, as an act of cowardice through which consciousness achieves its own self-destruction and hence brings about its cherished goal of coinciding with itself, that is to say, of transforming itself from a subject into an object or thing. Once again the substitution of *in order to* for *because of* makes all the difference to the analysis.

(a) The Rhetoric of Racism. I have so far suggested that racism is a source of security. This security is at least partly derived from the pseudo-scientific character of racist beliefs, which tends to invest them with the illusion of certainty. More specifically, by presenting such prejudices under the category of science, they cease to be merely subjective preferences, attitudes for which I must assume personal responsibility, and become instead objective facts which have been derived from an external, anonymous authority for which no single individual can ever be held responsible. In racism, one only believes what one is compelled to believe by the facts.[5]

In transforming one's prejudices into scientific beliefs, then, one places oneself squarely within the protective custody of determinism. But determinism is the very antithesis of morality. In moral situations I am required to make choices on my own authority, and such evidence as I require to support my actions is not always at hand. In the moral realm I am constantly required to question and evaluate my beliefs. In racism, however, I conveniently *avoid* the anguish of freedom by endowing my beliefs with scientific certainty. This, of course, is not only bad morality, it is bad science as well. In keeping with the whole character of racism, even its scientific pretentions are corrupt.

The racist has convinced himself that he believes only what he sees. He believes his attitudes are nothing more than the natural effects of pre-existing causes. They simply correspond with the facts as they are. "I hate Jews because they are greedy, mercenary, and so on." "I hate Negroes because they are dirty, stupid, barbaric, and so on." "I hate French Canadians because they are lazy, irresponsible, and so on." But in persisting in this behavior, the racist indulges himself in a ritual of bad faith or self-deception. It is the bad faith of surreptitiously endowing the world with qualities that necessarily place it beyond the realm of responsibility, and then convincing oneself that one's inability to feel responsible toward it is determined by the objective facts of the situation.

But this is really a kind of paranoia. I blame my behavior and my attitudes on the object. It never occurs to me that I am the source of my own behavior. The truth is, however, that the facts to which we appeal in order to justify our attitudes mean nothing until they are interpreted by criteria that we bring with us. The so-called facts we meet with, we ourselves place there, and then deceive ourselves into believing they existed all along and that we are simply compelled to accept them.

(b) The Morality and Ontology of Racism. One of the most acute analyses of the phenomenon of racism as an escape from the requirements of being human is Sartre's *Anti-Semite and Jew*.[6] In this book Sartre describes racism as a form of bad faith which seeks security through anonymity and loss of individuality. To judge the other as a Negro or a Jew is simply to classify him, to subsume him under an abstract general rule. It is to answer the question, How shall I deal with that man?, without thinking it out for yourself. I shall deal with him as a Jew—which is to say, I shall refuse to deal with him at all. Since Jews and Negroes are less than human, I do not feel threatened in their presence. In their presence I am

no longer required to be an individual. I have obliterated their individuality in order to negate my own individuality. In treating the other as a mere object, I become myself an object. For in branding him as a Jew or Negro, I bring him under a code that has a collective origin. I become part of an anonymous crowd. My attitudes and beliefs are vindicated not only by the objective facts of the case but also by the consensual validation of the many others who believe as I do —and we all believe together that we are compelled to our unanimous verdict by the brute facts of nature.

Through prejudice, the racist seeks out the protective community of men of bad faith who reinforce each other through a collective uniformity of behavior. Sartre's own description of the antisemite is worth quoting in full. The racist, writes Sartre, is a man who has chosen to reason falsely.

> How can one choose to reason falsely? It is because of a longing for impenetrability. The rational man groans as he gropes for the truth; he knows that his reasoning is no more than tentative, that other considerations may supervene to cast doubt on it. He never sees very clearly where he is going; he is "open"; he may even appear to be hesitant. But there are people who are attracted by the durability of a stone. They wish to be massive and impenetrable; they wish not to change. Where, indeed, would change take them? We have here a basic fear of oneself and of truth. What frightens them is not the content of truth, of which they have no conception, but the form itself of truth, that thing of indefinite approximation. It is as if their own existence were in continual suspension. But they wish to exist all at once and right away. They do not want any acquired opinions; they want them to be innate. Since they are afraid of reasoning, they wish to lead the kind of life wherein reasoning and research play only a subordinate role, wherein one seeks only what he has already found, wherein one becomes only what one already was. This is nothing but passion. Only a strong emotional bias can give a lightning-like certainty; it alone can hold reasoning in leash; it

alone can remain impervious to experience and last for a whole lifetime.[7]

This man fears every kind of solitude, that of the genius as much as that of the murderer; he is the man of the crowd. However small his stature, he takes every precaution to make it smaller, lest he stand out from the herd and find himself face to face with himself. He has made himself [prejudiced] because [in prejudice] one cannot be alone. The phrase "I hate the Jews" is one that is uttered in chorus; in pronouncing it one attaches himself to a tradition and to a community—the tradition and community of the mediocre.[8]

Sartre makes another point about the morality of prejudice. Being an individual, he argues, involves learning to distinguish between good and evil. But such distinctions must be made in fear and trembling, for there is no guarantee that our decisions in such matters are beyond question. In matters of morality there is no absolute certainty. But one can through bad faith transform the world into the kind of place in which certainty is now possible. Prejudice, for example, provides a definitive answer to the question, What is evil? Jews and Negroes are evil, therefore let us eliminate them. To eliminate an evil is to perform a good. There is no longer any necessity to think one's way toward good. Good is automatically realized through the elimination of what is recognizably and indisputably evil, like Jews and Negroes. Again I quote directly from Sartre:

The advantages of this position are many. To begin with, it favors laziness of mind. . . . The anti-semite understands nothing about modern society. He would be incapable of conceiving of a constructive plan; his action cannot reach the level of the methodical; it remains on the ground of passion. To a long-term enterprise he prefers an explosion of rage analogous to the running amuck of the Malays. His intellectual activity is confined to *interpretation;* he seeks in historical events the signs of the presence of an evil power. Out of this spring those childish and elaborate fabrications which give him his resemblance to the extreme paranoiacs. . . . [But] above all, this naive dualism is reassuring to the anti-semite himself. If all he has to do is to remove evil, that means that the Good is already *given*. He has no need to seek it in anguish, to invent it, to scrutinize it patiently when he has found it, to prove it in action, to verify it by its consequences, or, finally, to shoulder the responsibilities of the moral choice he has made.

It is not by chance, then, that the great outbursts of anti-semitism [as indeed any other form of racism] conceal a basic optimism. The anti-semite has cast his lot for Evil so as not to have to cast it for Good. The more one is absorbed in fighting evil, the less one is tempted to place the Good in question. One does not need to talk about it, yet it is always understood in the discourse of the anti-semite and it remains understood in his thought. When he has fulfilled his mission as a holy destroyer, the Lost Paradise will reconstitute itself. For the moment so many tasks confront the anti-semite that he does not have time to think . . . and each of his outbursts of rage is a pretext to avoid the anguishing search for the Good.[9]

I regard this kind of thinking as an example of "magicalism" —although psychiatrists, as Sartre himself suggests, might prefer to call it paranoia. There is something magical and paranoiac about believing that one need only eliminate evil to bring about good—which completely ignores the fact that the good society is the product of a positive effort to integrate one's inner self with the outer world.

I began this discussion by describing racism as a kind of faith or passion which provides the individual with a certain measure of security, and I have concluded with an analysis of racism as a kind of moral weakness—the sort of behavior engaged in by a man who seeks to flee from the responsibility of being human.

The first point I tried to make was that the racist seeks a scientific basis for his beliefs in order to derive them from an objective authority, the facts of nature. This he does, however, only by committing a series of "logical howlers" which constitute an abuse of the very principles of scientific reasoning. In the light of what I said about the morality and ontology of racism, however, these logical errors emerge as something *more* than mere mistakes. There is something almost deliberate about them. It is not simply that I become a racist through mistakes in reasoning, it is rather that I conveniently make mistakes in reasoning in order to be a racist. My choice to be a racist is prior to the logical structure of my reasoning. What I need to examine, therefore, is not simply my logic but my character.

Now I will admit that the relation between my behavior and my character is a problem to be further discussed. It is not always clear whether I am the kind of person I am because of the way I behave, or whether I behave as I do because I am a certain kind of person. But I have suggested, with Sartre, that the intelligible structure of man's behavior is derived from certain fundamental ontological features of the human condition, foremost among which is a kind of universal need to escape from the anguish of being genuinely human.

Finally, let me stress again that to examine racism as a phenomenon related to the human condition is not to minimize the importance of the causal or functional analysis of racism, which is an attempt not only to trace its origins but to explain how it functions as a social and psychological mechanism. The phenomenological analysis of racism is specifically an attempt to answer the question, What must be the nature of man *qua* man that he is capable of such behavior? Or, to put it another way, what can we say about the concept of man which conveys the existential significance of the phenomenon of racism? To view social phenomena in this way is to draw attention to the various philosophies of human nature that underlie our empirical study of human behavior. The phenomenon of racism thus points the way to the phenomenon of man. In attempting to answer the question, What is racism?, we are again confronted with the question, Who is Man?

2. MAGICALISM AND THE APOCALYPTIC ESCAPE FROM FREEDOM

The same kind of magicalism and paranoia that operates in racism underlies a host of other activities in which we are constantly engaged; such as, for example, blaming the environment for all of our difficulties and pretending that good will automatically come into existence once we eliminate social evils—or, more importantly, exhausting our energies in fighting communism, as though with the elimination of communism from the world virtue will once again reign supreme.

Take the tendency to stress the importance of social reform as a necessary condition of happiness. Isn't this just a convenient way of minimizing our own personal involvement in life? We demand the total reform of society. But this is impossible and beyond the capacity of any single individual. You can't fight city hall, we say: with the result that we do nothing. Complaining becomes a substitute for positive action.

Or again, think about how we deal with problems like air pollution, crime, and delinquency. Instead of dealing with such problems directly, we put them into the hands of a committee which studies the problem for a while and then reports back on its findings—with the usual result that a new committee is formed to continue the inquiry. And while the problem is being carefully studied, the rest of us behave as though it is actually being solved. I sometimes wonder whether we think that if the committee works hard enough the problem will just go away and vanish. Is this an example of scientific or magical thinking? I think the tendency to place our problems in the hands of experts instead of dealing with them directly does smack somewhat of the magical thinking that we all believe we have left far behind.

According to Sartre, and I would agree with him on this

point, all of these forms of behavior, including the surrender of freedom to totalitarianism, are patterns of bad faith which have their origin in the ontological predisposition to escape from freedom. Sartre's portrait of the individual who indulges himself in bad faith is compelling. He is a coward. He is afraid of himself and of his own consciousness; of his liberty, of his instincts, of his responsibilities; of solitude and of change, of society and of the world. He is a coward who does not want to admit his cowardice to himself; a murderer who represses and censures his tendency to murder without being able to hold it back, yet who dares to kill only in effigy or when protected by the anonymity of the mob; a malcontent who dares not revolt from fear of the consequences of his rebellion. In espousing racism, anti-communism, or any other form of prejudice, for that matter, he does not simply adopt an opinion; he chooses the permanence and impenetrability of a stone, the total irresponsibility of the warrior who obeys his leaders and pretends that he no longer acts but only co-acts. Such a man is consumed by a passion to be anything: anything, that is, except a man.

But, Sartre warns, although a man is free to indulge himself in patterns of bad faith through which he seeks to transform himself from a subject into an object and escape the anguish of being human, in this effort he can never succeed. Every such effort is in vain. The result of the surrender of freedom is that man will be consumed by the very forces through which he seeks salvation. Bad faith is implicitly self-betrayal. It leads inevitably to an imprisonment from which there is "No Exit."

What, then, does the Sartrian image of man mean to us with respect to the attitude we take toward the future? It means at least this much, that we must learn to live under the threat of disaster and still say "Yes!" to life. To exist in our world is to exist in the shadow of apocalypse. The apocalyptic vision has given rise to new modes of consciousness and imagination: it has produced a literature of violence and disaster, a theatre of the absurd, and a poetry of silence. Paul Goodman suggests that the psychological experience of apocalypse has produced at least two discernible ways of coping with the anomie of powerlessness to which it gives rise.[10] There is, first of all, the healthy revolt of creative disorder and civil disobedience which is a genuine expression of moral outrage, and which can also be viewed as an expression of *eros*. Through such acts of existential revolt, men seek to transform the universe into a theatre of unending creativity.

But man is also the being who, when he expects disaster, will seek to bring it about. This is the basis of what Goodman calls "explosive apocalypse," a pathological revolt of pure nihilism, which includes such phenomena as racism and many other forms of bad faith. And so Goodman urges us to the revolt of creative disorder before the psychology of the situation drives us helplessly into the nihilism of explosive apocalypse.

But I would urge that we think seriously before taking Goodman's advice, and the advice of others like Stokely Carmichael, Frantz Fanon, and Andrew Kopkind, to name only a few of those who have recently promoted the idea that violence is the only effective expression of moral outrage. The nihilistic undertones of this kind of advice are of course typically couched in a rhetoric which cannot but appeal to the hearts of all who really care about the plight of modern man. Thus Kopkind implores:

> It is not a time for reflection, but for evocation. The responsibility of the intellectual is the same as that of the street organizer, the draft resister, the Digger; to talk *to* people, not *about* them. The important literature now is the underground press, the speeches of Malcolm, the works of Fanon, the songs of the Rolling Stones and Aretha Franklin. The rest all sounds like the Moynihan Report and *Time*-Essay, explaining everything, understanding nothing, changing no one.[11]

But the rhetoric soon wears thin when it becomes necessary

to state specifically what shall be evoked: not love and non-violence and rule of law, or what humanists like to call the "Judaeo-Christian tradition." These are basically the demands of the very oppressors of society whom we all strive to unseat. The truth is, according to Kopkind—and he seems here to speak for the majority of those who espouse the philosophy of the New Left—"Morality, like politics, starts at the barrel of a gun." [12]

The statement is not simply a metaphor of revolt, it is an invitation to mutiny.

Is there not, therefore, an implicit danger in this kind of thinking which needs to be brought to the surface? To begin with, it is a pure confession of failure, a total eclipse of political and social imagination. In the second place, the distinction between the *morality* of violence and the *pornography* of violence is not so clear-cut. If man were an angel led astray by the evils of society, the program of creative disorder might well achieve some purpose. But if, as I have argued, following Plato, Freud, and Sartre, the pursuit of violence has its origin in man himself, then what is to prevent us from becoming victims of the very instruments through which we seek to reform society? Tell me, Messrs. Goodman, Carmichael, and Kopkind, what is to prevent you and your followers from coming to enjoy the effects of disorder to the point where you might be reluctant to change, even after you have made your point and scored your victory? If we decide to meet violence with violence, what assurance do we have that the experience of power—call it Black or White or whatever you want—which the use of that violence carries with it, will not become a primary drive which now seeks every excuse to be satisfied? If man is the source of negativity in the world, it is a short run from the life of creative disorder to the psychology of explosive apocalypse, from Black Power and civil disobedience to the pornographic enjoyment of power.

I want to make it quite clear that I am in no way seeking

to impugn the integrity of this concept of revolt, nor to question its legitimacy as an expression of moral outrage. And I am most certainly not condoning the injustices that Goodman and Carmichael attack. But I want to be sure that those of us who share the feeling of moral outrage have thought our way to a decision before embarking on a course of action that may well infect us with the same disease of power we are attacking.

Goodman defends the legitimacy of creative disorder and civil disobedience on the grounds that the state is after all a process, which is always in a kind of regulated permanent revolution. He also points out that such action revives the belief that the community is one's own and that one has influence: all of which curbs the anomie of powerlessness which is the source of explosive apocalypse.

> As the complexity, delays, and distance of ordinary political processes become greater, while often the tension of problems becomes worse, it is inevitable that spirited people will resort to various degrees of protest and civil disobedience. . . . But if place is allowed for "creative disorder" . . . there is less tension, less resignation, and more likelihood of finding social, economic, and political expedients to continue with. . . . How to encourage this rather than render it destructive by disregarding the need for it or even exacting draconian penalties to stamp it out? . . . This populism is called lawlessness, but, as I shall argue . . . it is the alternative to anomie and crime.[13]

Goodman himself anticipates the question, But how do you distinguish between sheer rioting and creative disorder?

> . . . in anomic circumstances it is hard to tell when riot or other lawlessness is a political act toward a new set-up and when it is social pathology.[14]

His answer is that pathological rioting is always in the service of the irrationality of the unconscious, while creative disorder is driven by reason and by Utopian goals.

I am often asked by radical students what I am trying to do with all my Utopian thinking and inventing of alternatives; perhaps the use of intellect is to turn riot into creative disorder.[15]

But surely the mere fact that one has invented goals does not prevent the unconscious from acting. What guarantee does a man have that the experiences encountered in the pursuit of his rational goals will not release unconscious forces which divert his appetites from the goals back to the experiences themselves, experiences which are essentially irrational, and which can only strengthen the demonic to the point where reason must now invent more goals in order to sustain the experiences? If in fact we even dare to admit that human nature contains an unconscious capacity for irrational behavior, then surely even Goodman himself will admit that between the "intellect" and the revolt of "violence" or "creative disorder" there must be a mediating factor which will prevent the intellect from being devoured by the experience of violence: so that the morality of violence does not become the pornography of violence. That factor can be none other than the "imagination of violence," by which the individual imaginatively lives through and hence transcends the violence and the evils that otherwise might choose more savage means of expression. Goodman himself writes:

> We Americans have not suffered as most other peoples have, at least not since the Civil War a century ago. We have not been bombed, we have not been occupied. We have not cringed under a real tyranny. Perhaps we would not ride so high today if we knew what it felt like to be badly hurt.[16]

But this is precisely the function of the imagination of transcendence as I understand it. Through the imagination we can in fact enter into the life-world of disaster in order to discover what it feels like to be hurt, beaten, and defeated. Through the imagination which expresses itself in critique, as well as in the various arts, the dimensions of human nature can be deepened. If through the use of imagination men can learn to transcend the disasters through which they paradoxically come to acquire their very humanity, then perhaps it will be unnecessary to confront these disasters in actuality.

3. THE LITERATURE OF DESPAIR

There is another way in which we can work to bring about the apocalypse of disaster. And that is through the *image* of ourselves we accept and which has a tendency to become a self-fulfilling prophecy. I am thinking particularly of the image of alienated man as portrayed in so much of the art and literature of our time: the image of man as helplessly impotent, passing from one form of self-deception to another, becoming more and more inarticulate, retreating deeper and deeper within himself, being lived more and more by his unconscious. Given what we know about man, it is not difficult to see how tempting it is to behave in ways which tend to confirm this image, thereby turning it into a self-fulfilling prophecy. It is much easier to conform to this image than to behave contrary to it. And as man is already predisposed to indulge in self-deception, and as he has a natural bent toward nihilism, we will never get rid of the merchants and pornographers of despair who stand to profit from man's inherent fascination with his own failure and weakness. While the weak among us retreat into violence, despair, and apathy, or into the far more appealing escapism of LSD, the merchants of despair lure us further and further unto the abyss by presenting this retreat as a new form of heroism and comic-tragedy. If man has lost the power to love and to be human, they say, it is for reasons over which he has no control, and for which no one, neither man nor God nor nature, is responsible.

"It is commonly assumed," writes the literary critic Robert Alter, "that to avow a lack of faith is a sign of honesty, and this is obviously often the case. But to absolutize a lack of faith in man and history and project it into literature is, for an artist, an easy way out, an escape from the difficult responsibilities of his calling. Through a habit of nervous laughter over the world's going to pieces, we titillate ourselves and at the same time imperceptibly inure ourselves to the prospect, so that it may become just a little more likely." [17] Alter is surely right. To justify failure as an inevitable outcome of forces over which we have no control is to practice the propaganda of irrationalism with a vengeance. While to present it as proof of the absurdity and meaninglessness of the world is an equally weak-willed indulgence in bad faith. In fact, there is nothing heroic or tragic in such retreatism: there is no dignity and no nobility in self-indulgence. There is no greatness in negativity. There is no humanity and no genuine artistry in a literature that amounts to nothing more than a pornography of failure that pretends to be great art.

The image of man condemned to death in a meaningless universe from which there is no exit is not an excuse to indulge in ritual acts of bad faith accompanied by requiems on the death of man and culture. Let us not confuse anguish with neurasthenia or skeptical paralysis, or turn the manly uneasiness of which the existentialists speak into some kind of pathological terror. But how, you will ask, in such an alien and inhuman world, can so powerless a creature as man preserve his aspirations untarnished? I think there is really only one answer. It has been given many times. Bertrand Russell expressed it well as early as 1901, in his famous essay "A Free Man's Worship." "In spite of death," writes Russell, "man is yet free, during his brief years, to examine, to criticize, to know, and in imagination, to create. To him alone, in the world with which he is acquainted, this freedom belongs; and in this lies his superiority to the restless forces that control his outward life." [18]

Russell's answer is essentially the same as that of the existential philosopher. Threatened by the inescapable limitations of his finitude, man is free because he can choose either to accept his fate with resignation or else to revolt against it. This revolt takes the form of a transcendental act of imagination and thought, an act through which we come to a lucid consciousness of the human condition. The classic expression of this idea is a remark by the seventeenth-century philosopher Blaise Pascal. "Man," writes Pascal, "is only a reed: the feeblest reed in nature. But he is a thinking reed. There is no need for the entire universe to arm itself in order to annihilate him. A vapor, a drop of water suffices to kill him. But were the universe to crush him man would yet be more noble than that which slays him. Because man knows that he dies and understands the advantage that the universe has over him. Of this the universe knows nothing." So, says Pascal, "let us not despair simply, but strive to think well. Therein lies the dignity of man. By thought he elevates himself and not by space and time." [19]

This remark by Pascal contains the whole essence of existential philosophy. Three hundred years after the death of Pascal, Sartre continues to write in the same spirit. Man, writes Sartre, is condemned to death in a meaningless universe. At the same time, however, he is condemned to be free: condemned to the formidable mission of being responsible for his own future, for making his death meaningful in the face of absurdity. This freedom is the real source of anguish. Anguish is not so much the effect of freedom as the consciousness of it. And far from being an obstacle to action, anguish is its very condition. More than this, it is an integral part of that crushing responsibility we all have toward each other which is the source of both our torment and our greatness. The salvation of man, writes Sartre, must therefore depend upon his ability to live without hope. For so long as he indulges in the therapy of hope, man is nothing more than a useless passion.

Why is it wrong to hope? Because hope can be the worst obstacle to action. Should one hope that evil will come to an end all by itself and without us? Hope is a ritual of magic which induces us to wait and merely fold our hands. But a man cannot will to act unless he has understood that he cannot count on anything else except himself, that he is alone, abandoned on earth by the very forces that created him, burdened by infinite responsibilities, without aid or support, without any goal other than the one which he gives to himself, and without any other destiny than the one which he forges for himself on this earth.

This intuitive knowledge of his situation is the source of despair. But it is also the source of transcendence. For just as anguish does not differ from the sense of one's responsibilities, so despair is only one and the same thing as "will-to-action." "With despair," writes Sartre, "begins the true optimism: that of a man who expects nothing, who knows that he has no rights and that nothing is owed him, who is happy to rely upon himself and to act alone for the good of all." [20] Such a man has learned to act not from hope but from the more profound basis of trust and faith. Like Abraham, whose anguish is a paradigm of existential courage, the existential Prometheus has become himself a creator of values. His is the responsibility not just for the discovery of meaning but for its creation as well. As Bergson said, at the end of his book *The Two Sources of Morality and Religion* (1932):

> Mankind lies groaning, half-crushed beneath the weight of its own progress. Men do not sufficiently realize that their future is in their own hands. Theirs is the task of determining first of all whether they want to go on living or not. Theirs is the responsibility, then, for deciding if they want merely to live, or intend to make just the extra effort required for fulfilling, even on their refractory planet, the essential function of the universe, which is a machine for the making of gods. [21]

It is to the imagination, then, and to man's capacity for creative thought that we must turn if we are to understand fully the dimensions of freedom and the possibility of the transcendence of despair.

CHAPTER SEVEN.
THE IMAGINATION OF EVIL AND THE TRANSCENDENCE OF DESPAIR

How we all love extreme cases and apocalypses. . . .
But . . . such convictions in the mouths of safe,
comfortable people playing at crisis, alienation, apocalypse,
and desperation make me sick. We must get it out of
our heads that this is a doomed time,
that we are waiting for the end,
and the rest of it. . . . Things are grim enough without
these shivery games.

Saul Bellow

If anyone in the world is custodian of the absolute truth,
it is surely not the man or the party which claims to
possess it. As for historical truth in particular, the more
one claims to possess it, the more one lies. In the end,
one becomes a butcher of the truth.

Albert Camus

It may be that in life . . . we reach heaven each by passing
through his separate hell.

Philip Leon

The central theme of all art, as Kenneth Rexroth once explained, is this: "Against the ruin of the world, there is only one defense—the creative act." [1] This is a profoundly correct outlook. Thrown into a catastrophic world, the artist finds art in a world of evil which he survives only to the extent that he uses his art to fathom the meaning of that evil. The artist is not simply a reporter who takes evil for granted and uses his talent to profit from man's inherent fascination for it. If a man is to be called an artist, it is because he has used his art not to exploit but to transcend evil. The way back to salvation is not to go mad and surrender oneself to evil, but to create. The creative act is the apotheosis of man; the destruction of creativity is therefore the greatest of all crimes. This is how the death of God comes about. It begins with man's destruction of his own creativity.

But this is precisely what is happening today. The life of creativity is slowly being infected by the propaganda of irrationalism, and the imagination, no longer informed by the *élan vital*, has lost its capacity to transcend despair and has become instead an imagination of disaster. The success of the propaganda of irrationalism in stifling the imagination is due partly to our own fears. We are afraid to be creative today because we are afraid to be individuals, afraid to be active in a conformist society that encourages total passivity. To be an individual in a collective society is to suffer a kind of madness. But to be part of it, which is normal, is to live without purpose, to worship platitudes and empty truths, to be mediocre, and to exist without love, which is hell. Hell is the suffering of being unable to love, and hell is the anomie and the powerlessness of living under the shadow of the apocalyptic vision.

Against this hell there have developed many forms of revolt: the nihilistic revolt of the emptied-out hipster and the social revolts of creative disorder, Black Power, civil disobedience, and so on. But the most profound attempt to restore the felt presence of the *élan vital* is the aesthetic revolt of the imagination which is slowly shaping a new environment for us to act in: an environment in which the revolt of action may conceivably be raised to a new level of possibility. For just as intuitions without concepts are blind, so action which is not informed by the imagination, even though it be driven by moral outrage, can barely be distinguished from blind rage. Only under the guidance of the imagination can the revolt of action transcend the limitations of the evils against which it protests.

If what I am saying makes any sense, then it follows that a philosophy of the imagination should precede a philosophy of action. The question, Who is man? is prior to the question, How should we act? Before a man can act effectively, his sensibilities and his humanity must be shaped by the imagination. The true path "from dissent to resistance" (which has today become the only course left for many of those who feel genuine moral outrage against the abuses of power which now threaten our society) must be bridged by an imaginative critique, if that resistance is itself to escape the disease against which it protests. By an imaginative critique I mean something which seeks not simply to assign responsibility for evil to the imperfections of society, but which seeks to locate the origins of evil in the ontological constitution of the human condition. And this is why I have gradually shifted the discussion from social pathology and the theory of action to the philosophy and phenomenology of imagination: all in keeping with my promise at the outset to inquire into the foundations of a new treatise on human nature which might better enable us to answer the question, What shall we do to be saved from our present distresses?

The imagination of transcendence, of which I am speaking, and which is an essentially creative act, is a more hopeful source of salvation than the programs of social revolt and social reform that critics like Paul Goodman and Stokely Carmichael advocate, for the following reasons.

In the first place, the revolt of action, as opposed to the metaphysical revolt of the imagination, is based on ideological commitments from which there can be no retreat. Of course, most of those who subscribe to this theory of revolt will deny that they are inspired by an ideology. It is, they will say, precisely the absence of an ideology which in fact defines the virtue and uniqueness of this outlook. But this is like arguing that there can be a presuppositionless philosophy. It is sheer rhetoric. The revolt of action is grounded in a very explicit ideology—the ideology of anti-ideology, or the ideology of moral anarchy. "Let us act first and think later." "This is not a time for reflection but for evocation." "Morality, like politics, begins at the barrel of a gun." But why the barrel of a gun? Why violence? Why even bother to revolt at all? Once these questions are answered, the outlines of the new ideology become obvious. It is not ideology that is absent here but "critique." If there is an alternative to ideology, is not a theory of pure action but a theory of action under the control of critique? As Albert Camus, whose thought is often cited by current leaders of the New Left movement, has himself put it:

> . . . the Left intellectuals . . . should begin to analyze critically the reasoning and the ideology to which we have so far subscribed and whose ravages we can see in the most recent historical development. . . . The Left is schizophrenic and should undergo treatment by pitiless criticism, by using the heart, by sound reasoning, and by a little modesty. Until considerable progress has been made on this work of reform, any group action will be useless and even harmful.[2]

Camus' advice, although originally aimed at the generation of young Marxists who flourished in the fifties, is just as relevant to the current generation of American leftists, and the leaders of the American New Left would do well to head it.

The difference between critique and ideology is analogous to the difference between an open and a closed system of values. In a closed system, action is forced into conformity with a fixed set of pre-existing values, which resist all efforts to change them. This is ideology. In the open system, however, the ideas and values that underlie that system are continually analyzed in light of the experience of trying to live according to them. The very effort to embody them in action, in other words, is a self-critical one: not just passive submission to an a priori truth, but imaginative and critical self-evaluation is the mark of the open society. In short, to live in the open society is to abide by a set of objective values, but always in a state of fear and trembling. This is critique. And critique is the only genuine alternative to ideology. For to reject ideology in the name of creative anarchy is simply to substitute one ideology for another—the ideology of private virtue, the absolutization of one's own personal goals. The latter gives rise to a tyranny of subjectivity as recalcitrant to the healthy dynamics of change as any tyranny hitherto conceived.

The revolt of action is, therefore, not a voyage of discovery undertaken in fear and trembling, but an attempt to implement an already defined but as yet uncriticized goal. Virtue is privatized and taken for granted; hence, one need only eliminate evil in order to ensure the continuation of virtue. But, more importantly, the revolt of action is waged at the same level of reality as the evil against which it protests, and so becomes a source of great confusion. To fight evil with evil is itself evil. It brings into play the very mechanisms against which it is reacting, to the point where the hunter can no longer be distinguished from the hunted. And under no circumstances can evil be redeemed by being brought into the service of a greater good. To do this is to indulge in bad faith. True, there are times when we must fight back; and at such times we often have no choice but to select our weapons from the arsenals of hell and our leaders from the devil's own academy. But at least let us not pretend that because what we do is for a good cause, our acts are any the less evil. As Pascal says, "Men never do evil so completely and cheerfully as when they do it from . . . conviction." [3] And, above all, let us not pretend that we can survive such an assault on our humanity without harm. To the extent that we are forced by the circumstances of history to defend our freedom by fighting evil with weapons that are themselves evil, we are confronted in a profound and compelling way with the essential paradox and absurdity of the human condition. As Emil Fackenheim once put it: "In the twentieth century, men—all of us—find themselves compelled to commit or condone evil for the sake of preventing an evil believed to be greater. And the tragedy is that we do not know whether the evil we condone will not in the end be greater than the evil we seek to avert—or be identical with it." [4] It is from this self-critical encounter with the finitude and limitations of the human condition that the true dignity of man first comes silently into being.

But the most critical question is whether in fact this is a time for evocation rather than reflection, and whether it is also true that in our time virtue can be evoked only through violence. Those who say "yes" are not beneath appealing to authorities outside their own milieu. The rebel's weapon is proof of his humanity, says Frantz Fanon in *The Wretched of the Earth*. Fanon is truly a philosopher of revolution, but his thought grows from the soil of colonial oppression which American culture has long since superseded. In Fanon, violence destroys an archaic authority in order to replace it with a new authority. For it is only by destroying the institution of colonialism that man legitimizes himself as man; and this he does by a law which is born each day under fire. In the fight against colonialism, then, it is perhaps true that morality begins at the barrel of a gun. But in this case the gun is a mere instrument, and not itself the creator of the morality to which it gives rise. The morality of socialism with which Fanon seeks to depose colonialism has already been thought through; it stands naked on the sidelines of history waiting for the owl of Minerva to take flight.

The problem in America, however, is not colonialism, and the new morality of the New Left is not therefore to be confused with the morality of socialism. The enemy in America is not a foreign colonial power, but man himself. American culture, having thrown over its foreign oppressor, now discovers the oppressor within. In American culture, mankind encounters the ambivalence of its very being as *humanitas*. If, then, humanity is to come to terms with its *daimon* it cannot be by destroying society. If from within the prison of our separate hells we are to legitimize and humanize ourselves through the birth of a new morality, that morality will come not from the barrel of a gun but from the imagination. The true revolutionary knows that the imagination too may be armed with loaded pistols. In certain circumstances, even to "speak" is to "fire." But the crucial point is that if one chooses to think and to act like a revolutionary, he must, as Sartre reminds us, "do it like a man," by aiming at targets— and not like a child, who aims at random by shutting his eyes and simply firing in the dark, perhaps for the sheer pleasure of hearing the shot go off.[5] That target, without which the revolution degenerates into sheer mutiny, is not given gratuitously; it comes into focus only through critique; it is as much a product of the imagination as are the weapons with which it will be destroyed. If, then, we fail, it will not be because we lacked bullets but because we lacked courage. We shall be as Alyosha Karamazov, seeking for immediate action and ready to sacrifice everything, even life itself, for it, but unhappily failing to understand that the real sacrifice is, as Hegel once said, "the labor of the notion." It is when this sacrifice grows beyond the strength of our exhausted imaginations that we seek refuge through the magic of violence.

We have learned that man is himself the source of the evil against which he is constantly struggling. And we have learned that evil can be overcome only through critical self-understanding. We cannot merely declare war against evil and hope to win. We can only transcend evil. The metaphysical revolt of the imagination will transcend evil because it alone produces an experience and an understanding of evil which is not itself evil. The imagination, not reason, is what finally separates man from nature. Surrounded by despair, the apocalyptic vision is superseded only by the prophetic imagination of transcendence. The goal of the latter, which is essentially a creative act, is a recovery of the totality of being, a recovery which is achieved by presenting the world both as it is in itself and in terms of its sources in human freedom. The ground of that freedom is the capacity for self-transcendence through critical self-appraisal. The imagination of revolt will therefore shrink from the idolatry of worshiping an ideology. Its task is not the adoration of an already existing idea but the celebration of ideas still in the making. The ritual celebration of an idea through critique aims at the renewal of a world hitherto paralyzed by crisis. Critique is therefore a synthesis of thought and action. It is, to borrow a methaphor from Sartre, a "festival" in which there is both sacrifice and generosity, in which the world is both removed and simultaneously returned as a gift. Critique, in other words, is in essence the subjectivity of a society in permanent revolution, and for this reason transcends the antinomy of thought and action. For it is only in an intersubjective community, whose very integrity and *élan* as a community is rooted in a spirited capacity to metamorphose through critical self-appraisal, that the imaginative critique of society can become an explicit condition of action. In such a society, the passion of violence will always be secondary to the more courageous "labor of the notion" without which man is but a useless passion.

2. THE IMAGINATION OF EVIL: FROM NIHILISM TO TRANSCENDENCE

The prophetic imagination takes a variety of forms. There is, for example, "the literature of silence," which includes the writings of Beckett and Camus as well as the messianic mysticism of writers like S. Y. Agnon and Eli Wiesel. There is also the theatre of the absurd, in which almost everyone writing today can somehow be placed. But finally there is something that I have chosen to call the literature of transvaluation, whose chief representatives are writers like Norman Mailer, Henry Miller, and Jean Genet. Of these expressions, the most problematic are the writings of Genet, and it is Genet's imagination of transvaluation that engages my interest and fascination. I say this not because his art is the most truthful or even the most beautiful, but because he is the most likely to be misunderstood, and because the significance of his art may well provide a clue to the meaning of the human condition. And so what I am about to suggest will, perhaps, seem shocking and disappointing to many. I may very well be mistaken in my judgment of Genet. But mistaken or not, my effort to come to terms with him arises from within the anguish of my own personal ordeal and proceeds from the conviction that, just as in the case of Camus' great novel *The Stranger*, it is important to decide whether the hero is a psychopath or merely innocent, so in the case of Genet we must decide whether he is a mere pornographer or, as Sartre claims, a saint as well.

It is, of course, easy to see Genet as a pornographer. His writings show a preoccupation with evil and disorder, with crime and violence, with every perversion imaginable to man. Not since the Marquis de Sade has there been such a literature of damnation. And to make it worse, his writings are autobiographical. He is himself the thief, killer, pervert, and homosexual that he writes about. But he is also an artist of great magnitude who has discovered a new form of imagination through which the evil consciousness is transcended by the self-consciousness of evil. Genet's artistry consists in his ability to make us realize that the evil he writes about is what we all possess but rarely come to terms with. No one who reads Genet and who understands him can continue in the

bad faith that we can exorcise our own evil by merely pro-
jecting it onto others: which is precisely what we do when
we vindicate our desperate claim to virtue by punishing the
offender. And no one who reads Genet can continue in the
bad faith of confusing virtue and moral goodness with
progress.

Genet begins with the fact that each man is a member of
a condemned society: condemned to evil by its own hypocritical practice of virtue, an act which has its source in the
predisposition of man "to-be-what-he-is-not" and "not-to-be-
what-he-is." Because society has counterfeited virtue by pretending to define it, the artist is compelled to express his outrage by deliberately attempting to reverse these arbitrary
patterns of thinking and perceiving. This he does by effecting
a series of transvaluations: good into evil, evil into good,
shame into glory, suffering into joy, death into apotheosis.
Sartre makes the point that Genet's writings are therapeutic.
By infecting us with his evil, Genet delivers himself from it.
Each of his books is a cathartic attack of possession, a psycho-
drama. With each work he masters increasingly the demon
that possesses him. And so, says Sartre, his years of literature
are equivalent to a psychoanalytic cure.[6]

Professor Tom F. Driver, a Protestant theologian and an
ardent admirer of Genet, thoroughly agrees with Sartre's description of Genet as a saint. Genet's purpose, writes Driver,
is not entirely selfish: it becomes Genet's intention, as if he
were a kind of messiah, to take the suffering of all upon himself.[7] He becomes the spokesman and the atoner for all who
are condemned by sharing their guilt and by carrying it to
its logical extreme. To take suffering upon himself is to fulfill
his self-chosen vocation of saintliness. Indeed, I would add to
Driver's point by inviting a comparison between Genet and
Orestes, the hero of Sartre's play *The Flies*. Orestes transcends the evil of his deed, the murder of his mother and step-
father, when he takes the guilt of mankind upon his own
shoulders and leaves with the furies at his back. The great-

ness of Genet, who emulates Orestes' heroism through the use of imagination, is that by sheer force of imagination he is able to transform experiences of degradation into spiritual exercises and hoodlums into bearers of the majesty of love. Imagination, as Driver puts it, is to Genet not only what therapy is to the psychoanalyst, but what prayer is to God.

The imagination of transcendence, as represented in the writings of Genet, has at least two functions. The first is to uncover, through an essentially creative act, what is implicit in every experience. The second is to fulfill the implicitness of experience by endowing it with concrete reality. The world of virtue is betrayed as being implicitly evil, while the world of evil is seen as a fulfillment of reality.

Genet has understood both the weakness and greatness of man. The weakness of man is not only his capacity for the pornographic enjoyment of evil but his predisposition to exorcise the evil within him by conforming to images of virtue and by punishing everyone else who refuses to conform. The greatness of man is his capacity for transcendence: his capacity to transcend the facts of his nature—lust, aggressiveness, unrestricted sexuality—by transforming these desires into love and by bringing his evilness into dialogue with the spirit of holiness. One lives at once in the sphere of the demonic and the divine, and salvation depends upon the imaginative effort to reunite what, by the accident of birth, culture, and progress, has been rent asunder. Creation and destruction are polarities of the same force; the act of negation is also the assertion of value. In the beginning, the spirit of holiness was outraged and compromised by the disembodied and artificial language of utility. That language must first be silenced before there can once again be communion with the holy. Silence, like prayer, is holy because it is the ultimate negation of false idols. Silence is the only possibility of a joyful affirmation of reality. We use language, you see, to counterfeit our experience of evil. We live in a world where the natural tendency of men is to counterfeit their encounter with evil either by indulging in it for a profit, or by inventing good reasons for justifying its presence in the world. But it is a far better thing to suffer the negativity and the absurdity of evil in silence while joyously celebrating in its transcendence. Silence is therefore the primordial condition of love because it is not preoccupied with the bad faith of counterfeiting evil.

Genet's message may be further understood by comparing it with Nietzsche's doctrine of total nihilism. By total nihilism, Nietzsche meant a nihilism of active and creative strength, as opposed to the negative nihilism of romantic pessimism, cynicism, and scientific atheism. Active nihilism is the nihilism of the man who, in spite of his acceptance of eternal return, the return of evil as well as good, is yet driven to say Yes! to life. This man is a man who can say Yes! without the aid of beliefs and false hopes. He is not a hero but an antihero. He has given up the nostalgia of permanence and the myth of progress. But only a man who has conquered, overcome, and transcended himself can acquire the "joyful wisdom" to desire the eternal return of all being and all beings, the eternal return of suffering as well as joy. Nietzsche's will-to-power is, therefore, the will to transcend the human, all-too-human existence of enslavement to false hopes and promises.

Nietzsche's total affirmation of reality, in all its shades and aspects, bears the features of a strange new theodicy, a theodicy which is no longer centered in the imitation of an objective transcendental reality, separated from human existence by the distance between time and eternity; it is rather a celebration in the transcendental subjectivity of man himself. Everything, writes Nietzsche, is only subjective, but it is all our work! Let us be proud of it.

Yet this joyful wisdom is acquired only in the context of misfortune. There is, writes Nietzsche, a personal necessity for misfortune. "Anguish, privation, destitution, dark midnights, adventures, daring risks and failures are as necessary for you and for me as their opposites; or, to speak mystically, the path to one's heaven leads always through the lusts of one's own hell." [8]

Genet has seen what Nietzsche was driving at, and what Freud too was saying, in his own way. It is that the angelic and Apollonian is also a potentiality of the bestial and demonic: which is, after all, what makes it possible for one man to feel compassion for another. And it is only when the demonic is clearly in focus that the beauty of the angelic can arise. It is not *in spite of* his irrationality but *because of it* that man is a god.

Bergson once said that the way back to reality is to destroy our perception of it, to do violence to our conventional habits of thinking and, by an act of imagination and heart, reverse the ordinary workings of the intellect.[9] The neo-primitivism of Norman Mailer provides us with just such an example of aesthetic distortion. Like Genet's exaltation of evil, and unlike the romantic individualism of Callicles, Julius Vander, O'Brien, and Adolf Hitler, Mailer's prescription for psychopathy must be taken as a poetic metaphor. It is not a manifesto for action but an imaginative invention. Mailer's complaint is that American society threatens to extinguish the animal in us. The soul of contemporary American man has been marooned in constipation, emptiness, boredom, and a flat dull terror of death, violence, cannibalism, loneliness, insanity, libidinousness, perversion, and mess. Yet these very fears are precisely the sources of the horrors from which men seek to escape. The lunacy of our world lies precisely in the fact that we are cannibals and perverts who pretend to be angels. What is lacking in our world is not violence, terror, and death but creativity and life. Thus, Mailer concludes, if one is to make one's way back to life and restore creativity to the world, the violence and irrationality from which we now flee must somehow be passed through, and digested, instead. In short, says Mailer, the way to transcend violence is to

commit it; get it out of your system once and for all. The
decision is "to encourage the psychopath in oneself,"

> to explore that domain of experience where security is bore-
> dom and therefore sickness, and one exists in the present, in
> that enormous present which is without past or future, memory
> or planned intention, the life where a man must go until he is
> beat, where he must gamble with his energies through all
> those small or large crises of courage and unforeseen situations
> which beset his day, where he must be with it or doomed not
> to swing.
> . . . The hipster, rebel cell in our social body, lives out, acts
> out, follows the close call of his instinct as far as he dares, and
> so points to possibilities and consequences in what have hitherto
> been chartless jungles of moral nihilism.[10]

But how does one commit violence? Not in *fact;* for to
commit it in fact is to surrender to it. To enter it through the
imagination, however, is to transcend it. The existential
moment is therapeutic precisely because it is imaginative.
Because it is imaginative, it permits the necessary psychic
distance without which there can be no transcendence.
Through the imagination one can endure all manner of sin
and corruption without becoming corrupt. Even the act of
murder can lead the imagination to the altar of holiness. In
the course of an interview, Mailer himself is reported to have
made the following statement concerning the idea of a brutal,
gratuitous murder:

> Let's use our imaginations. It means that one human being has
> determined to extinguish the life of another human being. It
> means that two people are engaging in a dialogue with eternity.
> Now if the brute does it and at the last moment likes the man
> he is extinguishing, then perhaps the victim did not die in vain.
> If there is an eternity with souls in that eternity, if one is able
> to be born again, the victim may get his reward. At least it
> seems possible that the quality of one being passes into the
> other, and this altogether hate-filled human, grinding his boot

into the face of someone . . . in the act of killing, in this terribly private moment, the brute feels a moment of tenderness,
for the first time perhaps in all of his experience. What has
happened is that the killer is becoming a little more possible,
a little bit more ready to love someone.[11]

Mailer makes a similar statement in *Advertisements for Myself*. The essence of the hipster's faith, he writes, is the belief
that

the real desire to make a better world exists at the heart of our
instinct . . . that man is therefore roughly more good than
evil, that beneath his violence there is finally love and the
nuances of justice, and that the removal therefore of all social
restraints, while it would open to us [by which I take it Mailer
means, to our imaginations] an era of incomparable individual
violence, would still spare us the collective violence of rational
totalitarian liquidations . . . and would . . . by expending the
violence directly [and again I take it that he means, by forcing
ourselves imaginatively to live through it], *open the possibility
of working with that human creativity which is violence's
opposite.*[12]

These terribly outrageous and monstrous statements are
profound. The entire history of mankind is a history of
redemption through atonement for murder. The very basis of
Christianity is a compassion which owes its origin to the
historic murder of a God: an act which has since become
the basis for a ritual act of atonement and redemption. The
imagination is what saves mankind from ultimate destruction.
Through the imagination the *fact* of murder is superseded by
the *ritual act*. Even the holocaust of Hitler's "inferno" can
be transcended by being imaginatively comprehended. When
men give up the bad faith of viewing this act as a distinctively
German one, an act for which Germans alone are responsible
(which historically may well be the case), and experience
it instead as a distinctively human event through which the
whole of man's nature is communicated, and for which all

men are responsible and must atone, then it will become part of the liturgy of evil. In celebrating it, the redemption of man may finally become a possibility. The salvation of our age, then, lies in nothing less than the speed with which the imaginative *celebration* of evil can supersede the pornographic *enjoyment* of evil through the exercise of power. Perhaps if men learn the proper employment of the imagination they may yet outgrow the necessity to progress through war.

In his preface to the *Phenomenology of Mind*, Hegel declares that the very survival of a culture depends upon how each generation relates to and relives its inheritance. That inheritance, even though it is already embodied in the culture of one's time, cannot simply be taken for granted. Its whole purpose lies in the force of its appeal to the generation to whom it comes as a gift, and its very efficacy and potency depend upon the style in which its incarnation into the here and now is finally consummated. That consummation rests on the ritual of labor through which the incarnated past comes to live once again in the present. Thus Hegel writes:

> . . . because the universal mind at work in the world has had the patience to go through these forms in the long stretch of time's extent, and to take upon itself the prodigious labor of the world's history, where it bodied forth in each form the entire content of itself, as each is capable of presenting it; and because by nothing less could that all-pervading mind ever manage to become conscious of what itself is—for that reason, the individual mind, in the nature of the case, cannot expect by less toil to grasp what its own substance contains.[13]

Or, to cite Goethe's later formulation of the same insight:

> What from your fathers you receive as heir,
> Acquire [i.e., earn] in order to possess it.[14]

To earn this legacy, however, does not mean literally to reproduce the horrors and errors of the past, with its virtues. History has already spared us this necessity. It is the imaginative reliving of the past to which Hegel refers, and, especially, the imaginative encounter with nothingness and evil. And not only the evils which have already appeared in history, but also the perennial possibilities of evil which linger in the depths of man's very being *qua* man. It is through the imaginative encounter with nothingness that man completes the self-making process which hitherto has proceeded through an *actual* encounter with nothingness. Thus Hegel writes:

> . . . the life of mind is not one that shuns death and keeps clear of destruction; it endures death and in death maintains its being. It only wins to its truth when it finds itself utterly torn asunder.[15]

Of course mind may, if it so chooses, simply turn away from the negative by either pretending that it is nothing or else dismissing it as a mere falsehood to be ignored, and being thus done with it, pass off to something else. But such acts of bad faith are not in fact the sources of mind's power and potency. On the contrary, mind acquires its power

> only by looking the negative in the face, and dwelling with it. This dwelling beside it is the magic power that converts the negative into being.[16]

The imaginative encounter with nothingness, in other words, is the source of the transcendence of nothingness in which it is not negativity *per se* but man's capacity for it that is transmuted. It is man himself and not evil which is redeemed through this encounter.

It is for this very reason that Collingwood has written in the *Idea of History*:

> Historical knowledge is no luxury or mere amusement of a mind at leisure from more pressing occupations, but a prime duty, whose discharge is essential to the maintenance not only of any particular form or type of reason but of reason itself.[17]

The importance of history is further demonstrated, according to Collingwood, by the fact that:

> The historical process is a process in which man creates for himself this or that kind of human nature by re-creating in his own thought the past to which he is heir.[18]

History, in other words, is not only a condition of the mind's knowledge of itself; it is at the same time a condition of self-making.

> Knowing yourself means knowing, first, what it is to be a man; secondly, knowing what is to be the kind of man you are; and thirdly, knowing what is to be the man *you* are and nobody else is. Knowing yourself means knowing what you can do; and since nobody knows what he can do until he tries, the only clue to what man can do is what man has done. The value of history then, is that it teaches us what man has done and thus what man is.[19]

> Since all he can know historically is thoughts that he can think for himself, the fact of his coming to know them shows that his mind is able (or by the very effort of studying them has become able) to think in these ways.[20]

> It follows that the knowledge [achieved] by historical inquiry is . . . knowledge of himself. . . . If he is able to understand by rethinking them, the thoughts of a great many different kinds of people, it follows that he must be a great many kinds of man. He must be, in fact, a microcosm of all the history he can know. Thus, his own self-knowledge is at the same time his knowledge of the world of human affairs.[21]

> The truth is that if the human mind comes to understand itself better, it thereby comes to operate in new and different ways.[22]

But what applies to history applies equally to other imaginative encounters, such as the aesthetic and religious encounters in which, to repeat, the perennial possibilities and dispositions of human nature are lived through and transcended. Just as the historian who has imaginatively lived through the past can better cope with whatever contingencies may arise in the future, thus preventing a nihilistic surrender to historical fate, so a man who has imaginatively lived through the demonic dimensions of his own nature is less likely to surrender himself to the pornographic enjoyment of evil when circumstances permit.

Looked at in this way, then, the imagination of writers like Genet and Mailer is neither pornographic nor apocalyptic-nihilistic. It is an imagination of transcendence which earns its positivity by "looking the negative in the face and dwelling with it." The greatness of such writers cannot therefore be diminished by those who are simply revolted by their message. One must understand the meaning of imagination if one is to understand the significance of a Genet or a Mailer. Their art is not merely pornographic precisely because it is a product of the imagination. And while the imagination may devote itself to evil, it cannot itself be evil. The theologian Tom Driver puts it well when he writes, concerning Genet:

> When pushed to the extremes of moral reality [the imagination] shows itself as the carrier in man of what is holy as well as what is evil. It becomes diaphonous, and one feels that he should indeed walk barefoot in its presence. It had been given to a pervert, thief, and coward named Jean Genet to come closer than the man of rectitude to the holy. Genet's head is full of violence, but his heart contains the rose of peace.[23]

It is interesting that this remark should come from a theologian. For there is something essentially religious about Genet and some reason to suspect that only deeply religious persons will understand what he is saying. The religious imagination is an imagination of compassion: it regards the evil person not as someone to be punished but as someone to be redeemed through love and compassion. It is the excessively rationalistic and abstract apocalyptic imagination that defines evil as an object of scorn, or as an incurable disease. The apocalyptic imagination is sober, passive, and detached. It seeks to reduce mystery to rational order. It sits in judgment, protected by certainty, and condemns. The religious imagination is active and participatory; it reaches out with compassion and responds with fear and trembling. It realizes that all judgment is self-judgment. But to live by the religious imagination is not only to participate in the world; it is to participate with the responsibility of one who is as much the *creator* as a *creature* of it. And, above all, it is to live as an individual rather than submit to the standards of public taste or the persuasive rhetoric of those in authority: to sustain, as it were, a constant critique of the canons upon which power insists.

The religious imagination, in other words, is prophetic and messianic. It is an imagination of transcendence. It seeks to restore the mystery of being, on the one hand, while at the same time forcing upon human understanding the paradox that while man is not the ultimate producer of being, he is nevertheless the director and architect of the world to which being gives rise; in which case, it is only man himself who can resolve the tension created by this paradox by bearing full responsibility before the object which has thus been laid bare. The prophetic imagination seeks both to restore the mystery of being and to reveal the limitlessness of man's freedom and responsibility. The judgments of the prophetic imagination have, therefore, no other substance than the subjectivity of human consciousness, from which source stem not only our *judgments* about the world but also the *renewal* of the world. But as in judging the world I tend also to renew it, the experience of this responsibility is onerous, and the burden of freedom entailed is too great for most individuals to bear. One therefore seeks to flee from its demands and to seek refuge within the protective custody of the community of men of bad faith who judge the world abstractly by ready-made rules and dogmas, and whose judgments are for this reason totally lacking in critical self-regard.

For the apocalyptic imagination, then, evil can be fought only by being eliminated, and the imagination can do nothing more than reflect, describe, and hence imitate. But there is a difference between the imagination as an imitation of (and hence submission to) reality and the imagination as celebration and transcendence: between the imagination as a mere consciousness of the world and the imaginative self-consciousness of the world. The former is essentially passive, rationalistic, and apocalyptic. But the latter is prophetic because it is active and creative. Through the prophetic imagination, the artificiality of experience is transcended. The prophetic imagination celebrates in the joyful presence of reality, in all its forms, and not just to the extent to which it conforms to false images of virtue and uncritically accepted dogmas. The prophetic outlook is therefore the noblest of all human postures because it exists without illusions yet rejects surrender, nihilism, and the paralysis of despair.

In his essay "Prophecy, Apocalyptic, and the Historical Hour," Martin Buber distinguishes between apocalyptic nihilism and prophetic messianism. The former manifests itself in a total withdrawal from a history that has become unbearable, while the latter is embodied in the more courageous posture that seeks engagement in even the most threatening of times. The prophets of the Old Testament, Buber reminds us, may have contributed to the apocalyptic vision, but they did so as prophets. They came not as oracles whose purpose was to *disclose* a predetermined future to which we are encouraged to submit. On the contrary, the outlines of future disaster are evoked not to curtail action but to encourage it. If such a future as the prophets disclose is indeed a real possibility, then all the more reason for us to exercise our freedom and responsibility. Thus, Buber writes, the task of the genuine prophet was not to predict but to confront man with the alternatives of decision.

> The prophetic faith involves the faith in the *factual* character of human existence, as existence that factually meets transcendence. Prophecy has in its way declared that the unique being, man, is created to be a center of surprise in creation. Because

and so long as man exists, factual change of direction can take place towards salvation as well as towards disaster, starting from the world in each hour, no matter how late.[24]

But, Buber laments, in addition to the prophetic tradition, the apocalyptic vision has given rise to a decadent, nihilistic imagination of disaster and despair, and it is this latter imagination which has taken hold of the world in which we now live. The result is that we are seized by a sense of powerlessness which encourages not transcendence but surrender, escapism, and moral decay. The fundamental presupposition of the imagination of disaster is the belief that everything has been predetermined and that all human decisions are only sham struggles: an attitude whose most vicious form is the cynicism that regards power as the only basis of justice and social change. Thus, the uniqueness of the prophetic imagination is its capacity and willingness to exist within the horizons of the apocalyptic vision without surrendering to it, to exist painfully in a world which by all the voices of reason is doomed to disaster, and still say Yes! to life.

3. THE POETRY OF SILENCE

The prophetic imagination can create the conditions under which man can learn to celebrate in the union of the demonic and the divine. But it cannot itself be a substitute for this celebration. Hence, the ultimate product of the imagination is a poetry of silence. Yet the meaning of that silence is profound. The literature of silence has broken down the barriers between subject and object, between truth and subjectivity. Hegel once said, "The owl of Minerva spreads its wings only with the falling of the shades." [25] Applied to the relation between art and experience, this means that the poet cannot draw the outlines of joy until it has become a concrete experience. On the question, What is good?, art is silent. That silence is an invitation for us to find the answer for ourselves. What offends most of those who react with hostility to modern art is not that these objects fail as works of art; it is rather that those who are offended are confronted with their own failure as human beings, their own failure to respond and react in a world in which they have become content merely to submit and look on passively. They are afraid to take that journey into the interior of one's own hell in order to emerge at the threshold of their salvation.

I am saying that the very possibility of our being virtuous presupposes a capacity for evil and depends upon the degree to which we can imaginatively "live through" and transcend the evil that possesses us. To imaginatively live through the ambivalence of one's essential nature necessarily leads to transcendence rather than negation. The cathartic effect of this self-encounter is an affirmation of one's creativity and humanness because the effort is already charged with these qualities. Transcendence, in other words, is not simply a *result* but a *presupposition* of the act through which it is achieved. It is only out of sheer ignorance that men propel themselves toward the negative; nihilism is a fate only for those whose lives revolve around the ritual of arrogant self-assurance, a ritual that is typically indulged in by the ignorant. The chief source of this ignorance is the bad faith of "the pursuit of happiness" according to the "right rule." But the path to self-knowledge is always in the context of despair. To travel it at all is to affirm one's courage and to define oneself as a project to be reached only through despair. For the man of existential courage, then, the encounter with despair ceases to be an obstacle and a source of disappointment. Neither does his virtue depend on a system of rewards and punishments, nor does his salvation lie in progress towards happiness.

For this reason I would reject any "repressive" theory of society and would favor instead what might be called an "expressive" theory of society. In the repressive society, education, in the broad sense of the term, is based on a system of rewards and punishments. In the expressive society, it would include opportunities for celebrating imaginatively in the drama of evil. The former is governed by a technology of socialization, which seeks essentially to adjust the individual to a pre-existing good. The latter, which is grounded in an ethic of humanization, seeks primarily to provide the conditions under which the individual creates "good" out of the chaos of his own nature. The paradigms of the expressive society are therefore to be found in art and religion. Through art the individual celebrates in the transcendence of evil *qua* individual. Through religion the ritual celebration of evil is communalized, and the imaginative products of art are now asserted as Truths to be lived by all men. But in the end, religion points back to art; the ritual transcendence of evil leads always to the poetry of silence in which the individual stands naked and alone in the presence of the infinite and must choose between waiting and acting, between surrender and creativity.

One of the most profound expressions of the poetry of silence is Beckett's beautiful play *Waiting for Godot*. The theme is emptiness. Two tramps are waiting in the middle of nowhere for Godot to come. He never does. That is all, and the point of the play seems to lie in its own pointlessness.

But this is not a nihilistic play. It can, on the contrary, be seen as a religious drama, as a drama of the religiosity of creativity and the creative transcendence of evil. To begin with, there is, as one critic has pointed out, an ambiguity in the very title, Godot.[26] In English the word suggests God; in French the closest words in sound are associated with vulgarity (*godenot, godichon, godelureau, godases,* i.e., runt, lout, boorishness, misshapenness). The inseparability of the demonic and divine, of good and evil, of banality and profundity, is a cardinal doctrine of Beckett's theology.

In the second place, there is ambiguity in the apparent pointlessness of the waiting. But the significance of this is finally revealed in the subtle disclosure that God is in fact present in the anguish of waiting itself. The point to be understood here is that God is not coming as a special event to offer us a deal, and to redeem us from a hostile world. God is already present in the world which is as evil as it is good—in which sadistic tyrants like Pozo torture helpless victims like Lucky in the presence of the curious indifference of men like Gogo and Didi.

But Pozo, Lucky, Gogo, and Didi are one and the same— man tortured and crucified by his own lack of humanity and in the presence of his own conscience weakened by disbelief. The resolution does not lie in waiting for miracles and divine intervention. Man does not transcend himself through waiting and hoping. This breeds "complacency," "magicalism," and, ultimately, "dehumanization." There is no virtue in simply waiting for what has been promised. Such lack of faith and courage is what makes the tramps what they are and gives a tragic quality to the play. What is wrong is the whole idea of waiting as such, waiting for signs and miracles, while all around reel shadows of indignant desert birds. What is required is the far more courageous act of assuming human responsibility for fulfilling the goals of man and God which are one and the same.

4. CREATIVITY AND TRANSCENDENCE

The relation between religion, creativity, and transcendence, which I am trying to explain, can be further explicated by turning once again to the thought of Martin Buber. In "My Way to Hasidism," Buber describes his encounter with the thought of Rabbi Israel Baal-Shem, the mystic founder of Hasidism. In the *Zevaat Ribesh*, the Baal-Shem-Tov describes the meaning of man's being created in the image of God. The man of true piety, he writes,

> takes unto himself the quality of fervor . . . for he is hallowed and become another man and is worthy to create and is become like the Holy One, blessed be He when He created His world.[27]

Buber's account of his personal response to this passage contains the essence of religious existentialism.

> Man's being created in the image of God I grasped *as deed, as becoming, as task.*[28]

From the Baal-Shem-Tov, Buber learned to find the essence of religion in creativity. As God made man, so man must remake and renew the world as well as himself. The essence of piety is the act of creation, not simply passive obedience to law. This activity, moreover, must be truly human, but is not to be identified with merely secular activities, such as the pursuit of material success, or the pursuit of power. The truly human act is an act of love, feeling, and intuition; it follows no law but that which stems from the radical uniqueness of each individual. It is, as Buber describes it, a "dialogue" in which each discovers himself through the "existential" presence of the other. In dialogue each explores the life-world of the other. By treating the other as a "thou," I bring his very being into the center of my own existence. The result is apt to be one of surprise, for in this act of intersubjectivity through which I appropriate the life-world of the other, I discover not only the other but myself; but the "myself" which I discover is a self I did not know, and so, in its first appearance within the horizons of my consciousness, it comes as a stranger. The "I-am-Me" experience which is occasioned through the encounter with the other is, therefore, essentially an act of creativity in which I virtually give birth to the self which I must now come to know. Each man, then, must learn to be an artist with respect to his own life. As Yeats said of the poet, insofar as he creates poetry,

> The fools that have it I do wrong
> Whenever I remake a song
> Should know what issue is at stake
> It is myself that I remake . . .[29]

so each man must say of himself as a man facing others in dialogue. And just as the poet is one who assumes the responsibility for bringing the products of the creative act to perfection in the form of a work of art, so the individual person must assume the equally onerous responsibility of bringing the revelation that stems from self-encounter to perfection. This he does by then acting on the world in a manner that is morally commensurate with his newly discovered, newly created self. To remake myself, in other words, is to assume responsibility for remaking the world as well. To feel responsible about the world is to be committed to acting upon it as I know myself to be, as a person, and not simply as one playing a role. Only in this way can I face the world as creator. To be created in the image of God means, therefore, to act on the world from a knowledge which proceeds from a self-knowledge that is itself the outcome of an existential-dialogical encounter with others. To know myself I must be prepared to love others.

But this existential-dialogical encounter, while creative and ennobling, is also not without despair and anguish. The encounter with oneself which the love of others occasions is an encounter that expresses the limitations, finitude, and negativity of men, as well as the beauty. It is an experience which reinforces one's sense of helplessness as well as one's sense of potency. And, finally, there is the anguish which accompanies the experience of freedom and responsibility toward the world, an anguish to which the dialogue of love inevitably gives rise. But then the significance of love does not lie in its capacity to facilitate an escape from despair. The meaning of love lies rather in its capacity to encounter despair with the purpose of transcending it. And despair is transcended not when it is simply eliminated or avoided, but when it is suffered in silence; when it is suffered through without loss of the capacity for love.

Buber's man of piety is the exact opposite of the hollow men who run our society and who have surrendered themselves to the propaganda of irrationalism, who are offended by modern art and who dismiss writers like Genet by branding them pornographers. Such men are experts in bad faith. They are magicians who skillfully transform the qualities of the world into a place where their surrender of freedom becomes respectable. They counterfeit the world in order to make it coincide with their own emotions. "There must be something wrong with such ideas," they chant, "because we find them repulsive and difficult to understand." They refuse to exercise independent judgment and prefer the safety of mediocrity.

But the ideas of writers like Genet are invitations to take the very steps that most men resist. If your experience is to be meaningful at all, it depends upon what you are prepared to contribute. Truth is subjectivity, and the greatest gains are made by those who are prepared to run the greatest risks. It is of course painful to discover that you have nothing to contribute. There is nothing so nauseating as the encounter with one's own nothingness. And so to escape you blame the artist, or become violent, or go mad, or simply feign indifference.

It is so easy to panic, to give up in despair, and to stop feeling. It is much, much harder to see around the unknown curve, to see beauty in ugliness, to see creative possibilities in apparent failures, to guess by means of intuitive wisdom just what the unborn thing we call our future will grow into. But this ability to transform despair into optimism is the mark of greatness. The great dignity of man, as Pascal, Sartre, and others have said, is his capacity to transcend his nothingness: to reach into his orphic depths and respond creatively.[30] The coward pretends to indifference; the opportunist and psychopath, by equating fleeting problems with the human condition, turn despair into an instrument of terror; while the pragmatist, by subsuming virtue under order, uses terror to initiate a process which leads inevitably to the judicial condemnation of the innocent.[31]

The creative person, however, neither seeks to profit from despair nor indulges in pseudo-humanistic mythmaking. He senses instead the vast, urgent hunger of men everywhere to become more human. This need can only be met through an imaginative exploration of the life-world of the human presence, which leads to a celebration in the thrill and mystery of that presence. The individual must therefore reverse the ordinary habits of thinking and feeling and view himself and others neither as victims of technology nor as potential objects of manipulation (lest these images become self-fulfilling prophecies) but as beings who *exist*. And what captures our interest about such beings as ourselves is the simple but astonishing miracle of each other's presence. But this presence becomes obscured for us by the routines of practical living and the clichés of everyday chatter; all of which alienates us more and more from the felt presence of the world as being. Only the imagination can restore the existential silence in which men face each other as persons, and this it does by recreating the situation of wonder and astonishment that defines the primordial condition from which we were once cast out and to which we are always seeking to return. The return to being through suffering and silence is the condition of man's ontological homecoming.

Our generation, then, has the task of living through despair without excuse. We have stepped out of teleology and natural law, not into chaos and emptiness but into a new creativity which must find its needed forms. Ours is the task, as Bergson says, of fulfilling the essential function of the universe, which is a machine for the making of gods. Yet, before man can complete his ontological homecoming and celebrate his reunion with the *élan vital*, he must first acquire that joyful wisdom that is the source of self-transcendence. As Nietzsche, Freud, Sartre, and Genet have discovered for themselves, and for all mankind, "the path to heaven leads always through the lusts of one's own hell."

NOTES

INTRODUCTION

1. On the origins and significance of scientism, see F. A. Hayek, *The Counterrevolution in Science*, Glencoe, Ill., Free Press, 1955, and J. O'Neill, ed., *Modes of Individualism and Collectivism*, The Hague, Mouton, in press. On the subject of a value-free social science, see Alvin W. Gouldner, "The Sociologist as Partisan: Sociology and the Welfare State," *American Sociologist*, May 1968.
2. See also Rollo May's "The Daemonic: Love and Death," *Psychology Today*, February 1968, and Ch. VI of his *Existential Psychoanalysis*, Toronto, C.B.C. Publications, 1967.
3. "Violence and Love," *Humanitas*, Fall 1966, p. 205.
4. *Ibid.*, p. 206.

CHAPTER ONE. THE PROPAGANDA OF IRRATIONALISM
AND THE CORRUPTION OF CULTURE

1. *Freedom and Culture* (1939), New York, Capricorn Books, 1963, p. 3.
2. *The Mind in the Making* (1921), London, C. A. Watts, 1929, pp. 28, 32.
3. I say mistakenly because if anyone thinks clearly about this line of reasoning he will recognize that someone's reasons for assenting to something may have nothing to do with its actual truth or falsity. And if you make your behavior the sole basis for determining the truth value of the image of yourself which this behavior expresses, you will very likely become trapped in a vicious circle. I run because I am frightened. And whether or not the basis of my fear is well founded, the faster I run the more frightened I become, while the more frightened I become the more justified I think I am in running—and so, the

faster I run. But what am I really running away from, a real object which I fear, or a fear which I first "objectify" and then project into the situation I am running away from?

4. *A Profile of the Negro American*, Princeton, Van Nostrand, 1964, p. 24.

5. *Universities—American, English, German*, New York, Oxford University Press, 1930, p. 15.

6. *An Essay on Metaphysics*, Oxford, Clarendon Press, 1940, Ch. XIII.

7. "Youth and Social Action: Perspective on the Student Sit-In Movement," *American Journal of Orthopsychiatry*, Vol. 33 (October 1963), 872–881.

8. *Ibid.*, p. 875.

9. *Ibid.*, pp. 877–878.

10. *Ibid.*, p. 881. See also articles by the same authors in the *Journal of Social Issues*, Vol. 20, No. 4 (October 1964), on the theme of "Youth and Social Action."

11. "The Ineffectuality of Some Intelligent People," *Commentary*, June 1962, pp. 482–483.

12. *Diagnosis of Our Time: Wartime Essays of a Sociologist*, London, Routledge and Kegan Paul, 1943, pp. 12–20.

13. For further discussions of the social role and responsibilities of the social scientist, see the following books and articles: B. Barber, *The Social Role of the Social Scientist*, New York, Collier Books, 1962; Raymond A. Bauer, "Social Responsibility or Ego Enhancement," *Journal of Social Issues*, Vol. 21, No. 2 (April 1965); Hubert Bonner, "The Role of the Human Sciences in the Dehumanization of Man," *Humanities*, Vol. 2, No. 3 (Winter 1967); Kenneth B. Clark, "Problems of Power and Social Change: Toward a Relevant Social Psychology," *Journal of Social Issues*, Vol. 21, No. 3 (July 1965); Lewis W. Feuer, *The Scientific Intellectual*, New York, Basic Books, 1963; Herbert C. Kelman, "The Social Consequences of Social Research: A New Social Issue," *Journal of Social Issues*, Vol. 21, No. 3 (July 1965), "Manipulation of Human Behavior: An Ethical Dilemma for the Social Scientist," *Journal of Social Issues*, Vol. 21, No. 2 (April 1965), and "Human Use of Human Subjects: The Problem of Deception in Social Psychological Experiments," *Psychological Bulletin*, Vol. 67, No. 1 (1967); Leonard Krasner, "The Behavioral Scientist and Social Responsibility: No Place to Hide," *Journal of Social Issues*, Vol. 21, No. 2 (April 1965); Floyd W. Matson, *The Broken Image*, New York, Anchor Books, 1966; Nevitt Sanford, "Social Science and Social Reform," *Journal of Social Issues*, Vol. 21, No. 2 (April 1965); John R. Seeley, *The Americanization of the Unconscious*, New York, International Science Press, 1967; Edgar Vinake, "Deceiving Experimental Subjects," *American Psychologist*, Vol. 9 (1954); Florian Znaniecki, *The Social Role of the Man of Knowledge*, New York, Octagon Books, 1955.

14. From "1 x 1" (ONE TIMES ONE)," in *100 Selected Poems*, New York, Grove Press, 1959, p. 90.

15. "A Very Stern Discipline: An Interview with Ralph Ellison," *Harper's*, March 1967, pp. 76–95.

16. *Ibid.*, pp. 76–77.

17. *Ibid.*, p. 77.

18. *Let Us Now Praise Famous Men*, Boston, Houghton Mifflin, 1960, p. 7.

19. *Ibid.*, pp. 11–12.

20. *Ibid.*, pp. 12–13.

21. *The Paranoid Style in American Politics, and Other Essays*, New York, Vintage Books, 1967. The paranoid style is a style of mind character-ized by the qualities of heated exaggeration, suspiciousness, and con-spiratorial fantasy, which tend to underlie extreme right-wing move-ments (but are not necessarily indigenous to right-wing politics). It is a style, moreover, which is not confined merely to the mentally ill. It is, says Hofstadter, the use of paranoid modes of expression by more or less normal, unselfish, and patriotic people that makes the phenome-non significant (p. 4).

22. *The Sane Society*, New York, Holt, Rinehart, and Winston, 1955, p. 15.

23. Thucydides, *History of the Peloponnesian Wars*, Bk. II, Ch. 4.

24. *Ibid.*, Bk. V, Ch. 7.

25. Thus Henry Steele Commager writes: ". . . a government and a society that silences those who dissent is one that has lost its way. . . . What is essential in a free society is that there should be an atmosphere where those who wish to dissent and even to demonstrate can do so without fear of recrimination or vilification. . . . When a nation si-lences criticism and dissent, it deprives itself of the power to correct its errors. . . . We do not need to fear ideas, but the censorship of ideas. We do not need to fear criticism, but the silencing of criticism. We do not need to fear excitement or agitation in the academic com-munity, but timidity and apathy. We do not need to fear resistance to political leaders, but unquestioning acquiescence in whatever policies those leaders adopt." *Freedom and Order*, New York, Braziller, 1966, pp. 291–294. See also the following works by Commager, whose voice has for years been a beacon in the wilderness of apologetics: *Freedom, Loyalty, Dissent*, New York, Oxford University Press, 1954; "An His-torian Looks at Our Political Morality," *Saturday Review*, July 10, 1965; and "On the Way to 1984," *Saturday Review*, April 15, 1967.

26. *The Hiroshima Pilot*, New York, G. P. Putnam's Sons, 1964, pp. 160, 312. For an interesting review of this book which raises some impor-tant questions about its alleged objectivity, see Edgar Z. Friedenberg, "The Question of Major Eatherly," *New York Review of Books*, April 30, 1964, pp. 4–5.

27. Preface to *Burning Conscience: The Case of the Hiroshima Pilot Claude Eatherly Told in His Letters to Gunther Anders*, with a fore-word by Robert Junck, New York, Monthly Review Press, 1962.

28. Typical of the rhetoric with which civil rights workers are often dis-credited is the now famous speech by Mr. Dickinson to the House of

Representatives, March 30, 1965, which can be found in the *Congressional Record* for that day, pp. 6113–6114.

29. The translation of Anders' letter, from which the following passages are taken, is alleged to be Anders' own and was first published in the now defunct Canadian review *Exchange* (December 1961), pp. 25–31. A corresponding translation is included in *Burning Conscience*, pp. 104–112, and it is to the latter that the following footnotes refer. Hence any discrepancy between the *Burning Conscience* version and the *Exchange* version may be regarded as a difference of translation only.

30. *Ibid.*, pp. 106–107.

31. *Ibid.*, p. 36.

32. *Ibid.*

33. *Ibid.*, p. 108.

34. *Ibid.*, pp. 108–109.

35. *Ibid.*, p. 110. A parallel incident is the recent case of a young Marine who claims to have resigned from the Marine Corps on a matter of conscience. The incident was first discussed by Paul Goodman in his controversial report "We Won't Go," *New York Review of Books*, May 18, 1967, pp. 17–20. This was followed by a letter from the young man in question to the editor of the *New York Review*, in which he discussed the circumstances relating to his resignation (September 14, 1967, pp. 33–35). The letter is a significant expression of the growing dissatisfaction of a large portion of the current generation of American youth with the bureaucratic mindlessness of the guardians who currently direct America's destiny in the world.

36. "An Historian Looks at Our Political Morality," *Saturday Review*, July 10, 1965, p. 18. *Freedom and Order*, p. 285.

37. Inaugural Lecture to the American Academy of Arts and Letters, Spring 1963. Cited by Samuel Hirsch in "Theatre of the Absurd," *Journal of Social Issues*, Vol. 20, No. 1 (January 1964), p. 59.

38. Collingwood, *An Essay on Metaphysics*, Ch. XIII.

39. *Speculum Mentis*, Oxford, Clarendon Press, 1924, pp. 33–34.

40. Translated by Richard Aldington, Boston, Beacon Press, 1955, p. 31.

41. For examples of this kind of political realism, one need only examine the various apologetics which have appeared in defense of the Vietnam war. Granted these have not gained the universal support of the intellectuals, many of whom at least claim to be on the side of morality. But any question as to whether this inversion of morality has occurred on official levels will be easily dispelled by examining a book such as *Air War Vietnam* by Frank Harvey, New York, Bantam Books, 1967. The importance of this book lies not in the author's views but in the attitudes which he reports to exist in official circles. See also Commager, "On the Way to 1984."

42. See *Autobiography*, London, Oxford University Press, 1939, pp. 48–49.

43. "An Historian Looks at Our Political Morality," p. 16; *Freedom and Order*, p. 280.

44. "What's Happening to America," Symposium, *Partisan Review,* Winter 1967, p. 52.
45. *Ibid.*
46. *The Moral Ambiguity of America,* Toronto, C.B.C. Publications, 1967, p. 65. An American edition is published by Random House. All references here, however, are to the Canadian edition. In this connection it is worth consulting Michael Harrington's *The Accidental Century,* New York, Macmillan, 1965.
47. New York, Atheneum, 1967, pp. 67–68, 365.

CHAPTER TWO. WHO IS MAN? NATURAM SEQUERE!

1. E. T. Campagnac, ed., *The Cambridge Platonists,* Oxford, 1901, p. 68.
2. The quotations from Tillotson and Kidder are cited by Ronald S. Crane in "Suggestions Towards a Genealogy of 'The Man of Feeling,'" *English Literary History,* I (1934), 228. See also Louis I. Bredvold, *The Brave New World of the Enlightenment,* Ann Arbor, University of Michigan Press, 1962, p. 64.
3. In *Rameau's Nephew and Other Works,* translated by Jacques Barzun and Ralph H. Bowen, Indianapolis, Bobbs Merrill, 1964, p. 186. It should be pointed out, however, that Diderot was somewhat inconsistent on the question of human nature. In his *Refutation of Helvétius' Treatise on Man* (1773–1776), he appears to have compromised his humanism and seems to accept the hypothesis that irrationality and vice may possibly have their origin as much in human nature as in society.
4. *Enquiry Concerning Political Justice,* ed. by F. E. L. Priestly, Toronto, University of Toronto Press, 1946, II, Bk. V, Ch. XXIV, 210–211. It must be remembered, of course, that for Godwin social reform means virtually the elimination of the entire complexity of government and the creation of a state of anarchy in which man's natural propensity to reason and to be creative is allowed to flourish, unmolested by restrictions, taboos, and all other such cumbersome apparatus.
5. Condorcet, *Sketch for a Historical Picture of the Progress of the Human Mind* (1795), translated by June Barraclough, New York, Noonday Press, 1955, p. 202.
6. "A Discourse on the Moral Effects of the Arts and Sciences," in *The Social Contract and Discourses,* translated by G. D. H. Cole, London, J. M. Dent, 1913, p. 152.
7. The emphasis, at any rate, should be placed on what the individual can do for himself. And in this regard there is no more important act than the pursuit of self-knowledge. The principles of morality and truth, writes Rousseau, are "graven on every heart"; in which case, he continues, need we do more to learn those laws "than to examine our-

selves and listen to the voice of conscience, when the passions are silent?" *Ibid.*, p. 154.

8. *Emile*, Bk. IV, translated by Barbara Foxley, London, J. M. Dent, 1911, p. 252.

9. *The Social Contract*, Bk. I, Ch. VII, p. 18. My italics.

10. *Ibid.*, Bk. I, Ch. VIII, p. 19.

11. *Pensées*, translated by W. F. Trotter, New York, Random House, 1941, Section IV, No. 277 (p. 95), No. 282 (pp. 95–96). See also No. 252 (pp. 89–90).

12. *Emile*, p. 249.

13. *Ibid.*, p. 253. My italics.

14. *Ibid.*, p. 255.

15. *Ibid.*, pp. 249–250.

16. See, for example, Kenneth Kenniston, *The Uncommitted: A Study of Alienated Youth in America*, New York, Dell, 1967, and Jules Henry, *Culture Against Man*, New York, Random House, 1963.

17. *Being and Nothingness*, Part One, Ch. One and Ch. Two, Section 1.

18. *Growing Up Absurd*, New York, Random House, 1956, pp. 10–12.

19. *The Moral Ambiguity of America*, pp. 12–13.

20. *Ibid.*, pp. 23–24.

21. *The Society I Live In Is Mine*, New York, Horizon Press, 1962, pp. ix–x.

22. *Ibid.*, p. x.

23. *Ibid.*, p. viii. For a further discussion on this point, see below Chs. Six and Seven.

24. *Must You Conform?*, New York, Grove Press, 1956, pp. 23, 26. See also *Prescription for Rebellion*, London, Victor Gollancz, 1953. A series of experiments conducted by Stanley Milgram between 1961 and 1964 tends strongly to confirm Lindner's psychoanalytic speculations. See in particular his exceedingly important article, "Some Conditions of Obedience and Disobedience to Authority," *Human Relations*, Vol. 18, No. 1 (1965), 57–76, which reports the results of experiments that inquire into the structure of situations in which one agent or authority commands another to inflict pain on a third. Milgram's conclusions are worth quoting in full. "The results, as seen and felt in the laboratory, are to this author disturbing. They raise the possibility that human nature, or—more specifically—the kind of character produced in American democratic society, cannot be counted on to insulate its citizens from brutality and inhumane treatment at the direction of a malevolent authority. A substantial proportion of people do what they are told to do, irrespective of the content of the act and without limitations of conscience, so long as they perceive that the command comes from a legitimate authority. If in this study an anonymous experimenter could successfully command adults to subdue a fifty-year-old man, and force on him painful electric shocks against his protests, one can only wonder what government, with its vastly greater author-

ity and prestige, can command of its subjects. There is, of course, the extremely important question of whether malevolent political institutions could or would arise in American society" (p. 75).

25. "Adolescents in Mutiny," *The Pocket Book Magazine*, No. 3, New York, 1955, p. 56.

26. David McClelland, "Some Social Consequences of Achievement Motivation," *Nebraska Symposium on Motivation*, ed. by M. R. Jones, Lincoln, University of Nebraska Press, 1955, p. 45.

27. *The Achieving Society*, New York, Free Press, 1967, p. 336.

28. *Ibid.*, pp. 336–390.

29. *Ibid.*, p. 392.

30. *Ibid.*, p. 340, 391.

31. *Ibid.*, pp. 393–394.

32. *Ibid.*, pp. 391–437.

33. "Achievement Drive and Economic Growth," in *The Roots of Consciousness*, Princeton, Van Nostrand, 1964, pp. 16–17.

34. *Coming of Age in America*, New York, Vintage Books, 1967, pp. 12–13.

35. Writing in 1930, Freud declared at the conclusion of *Civilization and Its Discontents* that "If the evolution of civilization has such far-reaching similarity with the development of an individual, and if the same methods are employed in both, would not the diagnosis be justified that many systems of civilization—or epochs of it—possibly even the whole of humanity—have become 'neurotic' under the pressure of civilizing trends? . . . The diagnosis of collective neurosis, however, will be confronted by a special difficulty. In the neurosis of an individual we can use as a starting point the contrast presented to us between the patient and his environment which we assume to be 'normal.' No such background as this would be available for any society similarly affected; it would have to be supplied in some other way. And with regard to any therapeutic application of our knowledge, what would be the use of the most acute analysis of social neurosis, since no one possesses power to compel the community to adopt the therapy? In spite of all these difficulties, we may expect that one day someone will venture upon this research into the pathology of civilized communities" (New York, Anchor Books ed., pp. 103–104). As for Freud's point about the criterion of "normalcy," which is clearly presupposed by such an enterprise, it seems that, as in the case of Erich Fromm, the criterion is usually derived from an a priori theory of human nature. Hence the recent popularity of social pathology has produced a renewed interest in theories of human nature, or philosophical anthropology.

36. *The Sane Society*, pp. 10–11.

37. "Disengagement: The Art of the Beat Generation," *New World Writing*, No. 11, New York, New American Library, 1957; reprinted in *The Beat Generation and the Angry Young Men*, ed. by Gene Feldman and Max Gartenberg, New York, Dell, 1959, pp. 366–367.

38. *Ibid.*, p. 359.
39. New York, Random House, 1962, p. 12.
40. Bk. VI, Ch. III, (i), New York, Modern Library, 1950, p. 387.
41. *The Sane Society*, p. 20.
42. New York, Holt, Rinehart, and Winston, 1941, p. 6.
43. *Ibid.*, pp. 12–13.
44. "The American Way of Death," *New York Review of Books*, April 28, 1966, p. 5.
45. *Marxism and Psychoanalysis*, New York, Monthly Review Press, 1960, p. 14.
46. New York, Macmillan, 1948, p. 89.
47. "Freedom and the Control of Men," *American Scholar*, Vol. 25 (Winter 1955–1956), 56–57. See also *Walden II*, Chs. 29 and 32.
48. *Sketch for a Theory of the Emotions* (1939), translated by Philip Mairet. London, Methuen, 1962.
49. For a further discussion of the hermeneutic technique, see Lionel Rubinoff, "Perception, Self-Making and Transcendence," *International Philosophical Quarterly*, Vol. 3, No. 3 (September 1967), and Paul Ricoeur, "Existence et Herméneutique," *Dialogue*, IV, June 1965.

CHAPTER THREE. TWILIGHT OF THE IDOLS

1. *The Joyful Wisdom*, III, § 125.
2. *Ibid.;* see also IV, § 285. In this passage Nietzsche discusses the implications of the death-of-God experience and exposes the essential ambiguity of nihilism as a source of transcendence as well as despair. Nietzsche writes: "Thou wilt never more pray, never more worship, never more repose in infinite trust—thou refusest to stand still and dismiss thy thoughts before an ultimate wisdom, an ultimate virtue, an ultimate power—thou hast no constant guardian and friend in thy seven solitudes—thou livest without the outlook on a mountain that has snow on its head and fire in its heart—there is no longer any requiter for thee, nor any amender with his finishing touch—there is no longer any reason in that which happens, or any love in that which will happen to thee—there is no longer any resting place for thy weary heart, where it has only to find and no longer to seek, thou art opposed to any kind of ultimate peace, thou desirest the eternal recurrence of war and peace:—man of renunciation, wilt thou renounce in all these things? Who will give thee the strength to do so? No one has yet had this strength:—There is a lake which one day refused to flow away, and there is a dam at the place where it had hitherto discharged: since then this lake has always risen higher and higher. Perhaps the very renunciation will also furnish us with the strength with which the renunciation itself can be borne; perhaps man will ever rise

higher and higher from that point onward, when he no longer flows out into a God."

3. *The Descent of Man*, London, 1871, 2nd. ed., 1888, Part III, Ch. XXI, General Summary. These are in fact the sentiments expressed in the very last words.

4. *A General Introduction to Psychoanalysis*, 1915–1917, Lecture 18, translated by Joan Riviere, New York, Washington Square Press, 1960, p. 296.

5. "A Free Man's Worship" (1902), in *Mysticism and Logic* (1917), New York, Anchor Books, 1957, pp. 45–46.

6. *The Heavenly City of the Eighteenth-Century Philosophers*, New Haven, Yale University Press, 1932, pp. 14–15.

7. *The Leviathan*, Part I, Chs. XIII and XIV.

8. *The Fable of the Bees* (1714), ed. by Irwin Primer, New York, Capricorn Books, 1962, p. 155.

9. *Ibid.*, p. 156.

10. *Maxims*, translated and ed. by Constantine FitzGibbon, London, Wingate, 1957. Based on the 5th ed. of 1678, Paris, Claude Barbin. Nos. 305 (p. 92), 78 (p. 47), 112 (p. 55), 237 (p. 79), 308 (p. 92).

11. Ch. V, Anchor Books ed., pp. 60–61.

12. *Gorgias*, pp. 482–484 (Sephanus pagination, any edition).

13. "The Second Coming," in *Collected Poems*, London, Macmillan, 1952, pp. 210–211.

14. London, *Bodley Head*, 1938, pp. 119–120.

15. New York, Signet Books, 1950, p. 200.

16. *Ibid.*, pp. 202–203.

CHAPTER FOUR. IRRATIONALISM AND THE
INVOCATION OF VIRTUE

1. *Republic*, Bk. I.

2. *The Discourses*, Bk. I, Ch. 9. "Nor will a prudent intellect ever censure anyone for any unlawful action used in organizing a kingdom or setting up a republic. It is at any rate fitting that though the deed accuses him the result should excuse him; and when it is good . . . it will always excuse him, because he who is violent to destroy, not he who is violent to restore, ought to be censured." *The Chief Works and Others*, translated by Alan Gilbert, Durham, N.C., Duke University Press, 1965, I, 218.

3. *The Prince* (1532), Ch. 18. *The Chief Works*, I, 64–67.

4. *The History of Florence*, Bk. III, Ch. 13. *The Chief Works*, III, 1160. For an important discussion of the significance of Machiavellianism, see Irving Kristol's "Machiavelli's Profanation of Politics," in *The Logic of Personal Knowledge: Essays Presented to Michael Polanyi*,

London, Routledge and Kegan Paul, 1961, in which Kristol suggests that Machievelli's political thought is virtually a form of "political pornography."

5. *Leviathan*, Part II, Ch. XVII.
6. *A Treatise on Man* (1772), translated by W. Hopper, London, 1777, II, 299.
7. *De L'Esprit* (1758), English translation, London, Albion Press, 1810, Essay II, pp. 184–186.
8. *Civilization and Its Discontents*, p. 40.
9. *Ibid.*, pp. 62–63.
10. *Ibid.*, p. 66. See also *Collected Papers*, New York, Basic Books, 1959, V, 281.
11. *Civilization and Its Discontents*, p. 68.
12. *Collected Papers*, V, 281.
13. *Civilization and Its Discontents*, p. 66.
14. Pp. 1–7.
15. P. 167.
16. See, for example, E. R. Dodds, *The Greeks and the Irrational*, Berkeley, University of California Press, 1951. See especially Ch. VIII, "The Fear of Freedom."
17. "Freedom and the Control of Men," p. 56.
18. *The Brothers Karamazov*, Bk. V, Ch. V.
19. See, for example, Plato, *Republic*. Adeimantus sums up the problem which Socrates must deal with if he is to undermine the appeal of Thrasymachus. "What argument, then, remains for preferring justice to the worst injustice when both common men and great men agree that, provided it has a veneer of respectability, injustice will enable us, in this world and the next, to do as we like with gods and men? And how can anyone, when he has heard all we have said, possibly avoid laughing when he hears justice being praised, if he has any force of character at all?" (366b, Stephanus pagination).
20. Scene 8. The above passage is taken from Desmond I. Vesey's translation, London, Methuen, 1963, pp. 76–77.
21. Munich, April 13, 1923. Reprinted in *Hitler's Words*, ed. by Gordon W. Prange, Washington, American Council on Public Affairs, 1944, p. 11; and *My New Order*, ed. with a commentary by Raoul de Roussy de Sales, New York, Reynal and Hitchcock, 1941, p. 50.
22. Essen, November 22, 1926; *Hitler's Words*, p. 4.
23. Munich, April 2, 1927; *ibid.*, p. 5.
24. Kulmbach, February 5, 1928; *ibid.*, p. 8.
25. Chemnitz, April 2, 1928; *ibid.*, pp. 8–9.
26. Munich, March 15, 1929; *ibid.*, p. 111.
27. Printed and distributed by the National Putnam Letters Committee, New York, pp. 18, 23–24. For a discussion of Putnam's brand of racism, see I. A. Newby's valuable study, *Challenge to the Court*, Baton Rouge, Louisiana State University Press, 1967. See also Chapter Six below.

CHAPTER FIVE. HUMANIZATION AND THE
EXPERIENCING OF MEANING

1. *The Informed Heart,* New York, Free Press, 1964, pp. 6–7.
2. Thus Karl Jaspers writes: ". . . in our age, when the old polarities
between the individual and society, community and collectivity are
being eroded, we pin our hope on the individual. Only the individual
can construct the true community which may one day spiritualize the
world of technology. . . . The individual is today charged with an
extraordinary task. . . . if the individual asserts himself, we may hope
that with the help of a reborn community, we will successfully avert
the destruction of mankind." "The Individual and the Collectivity,"
Noonday 1, New York, 1958, pp. 61–62.
3. *Republic,* 493 (Stephanus pagination, any edition). See also the following example from Rollo May's C.B.C. lectures on *Existential Psychotherapy,* Toronto, C.B.C. Publications, 1967. In the course of his research on anxiety, May set out to study anxiety in a group of unmar-
ried mothers. He began with the hypothesis that the predisposition
toward anxiety in individuals would be proportionate to how much
they had been rejected by their mothers. But in fact only half the
girls fitted the hypothesis. The others did not conform at all—particularly the girls from Harlem and the Lower East Side who had grown
up in poverty-stricken homes but who showed no traces of manifest or
even residual anxiety. A solution to the difficulty came when May
suddenly realized the difference between the life-world of the middle
class (whose girls tended to conform to the hypothesis) and the life-
world of the lower class (whose girls tended not to conform to the
hypothesis). May's own words speak for themselves. "I saw . . . that
it is not rejection by the mother that is the original trauma which is
the source of anxiety; *it is, rather, rejection that is lied about.* The
proletarian mothers rejected their children, but they never made any
bones about it. The children knew they were rejected and they went
out on the streets and found other companions. They knew their
world; there was no subterfuge about their situation, and therefore
they could orient themselves. The middle-class girls, on the other hand,
were always lied to by their mothers. The middle-class girls were rejected by their mothers, but the mothers pretended they loved them
and this was really their source of anxiety, not the sheer rejection. . . .
Anxiety comes from something different than sheer rejection: it comes
from not being able to know the world you are in, not being able to
orient yourself in your own existence" (p. 44).
4. *Republic,* 363–367.
5. *Ibid.,* 365e.

6. *Memoirs of a Dutiful Daughter*, Cleveland, World Publishing Co., 1959, pp. 206–207.

7. Cited by T. V. LoCicero in "The Murder of Rabbi Adler," *Commentary*, June 1966, p. 52.

8. *Ibid.*, p. 53.

9. *Phaedo*, 97c–99c.

10. *Republic*, 443d–e.

11. *Theatetus*, 177a.

12. In fact, one might go so far as to argue that the recent acceleration of lawlessness in American society, such as, for example, the riots in Negro ghettos, is a typically American way of reacting to a hostile environment. The Negro is simply bringing the traditional American custom of progress through violence to its logical conclusion.

13. *The Brothers Karamazov*. The above and following passages are taken from the translation by Constance Garnett, New York, Random House, 1950, p. 25. According to LoCicero, this very passage was underlined by Richard Wishnetsky, who also had inscribed in the margin, "Me."

14. *The Brothers Karamazov*, p. 25. This part of the passage, as LoCicero points out, had apparently escaped Wishnetsky's notice.

CHAPTER SIX. THE APOCALYPTIC VISION AND THE
NIHILISM OF DESPAIR

1. *Being and Nothingness*, translated by Hazel Barnes, New York, Philosophical Library, 1956, Part One, Ch. Two, § II, p. 58.

2. *Notes from the Underground*, Part I, § VIII.

3. *Being and Nothingness*, Part I, Ch. 2, § 1, p. 49.

4. "What's Happening to America," p. 52.

5. Examples of attempts to defend racism on scientific grounds are such books as *Race and Reason* by Carleton Putnam, Washington, Public Affairs Press, 1961, and *The Biology of the Race Problem* by Wesley Critz George, a report prepared by commission of the Governor of Alabama, 1962. Other examples can be found in the writings of such well-known scientists and scholars as Henry E. Garrett, R. Ruggles Gates, Ernest Van den Haag, A. James Gregor, and Robert T. Osborne. Each of the above is a member of the IAAEE (International Association for the Advancement of Ethology and Eugenics). Although the association is ostensibly dedicated to promoting the unbiased and unprejudiced study of race, a convincing case has been made by I. A. Newby to show that the IAAEE has done more than any other organization to facilitate the use of science and scientific literature by segregationists and anti-Negro racists. In support of this charge one need only examine the contents of the various monographs, reprints, and issues of the journal *Mankind Quarterly* sponsored by the

IAAEE. Newby's book, *Challenge to the Court,* is the most serious effort to date to assess the implications and social significance of pseudo-scientific racism. Its main point is that we can no longer afford the luxury of dismissing racism as an attitude held only by a few cranks and fanatics, which because of its disreputable origins is bound to give way to the appeal to reason. "Regardless of the offensiveness of the ideas they profess and the policies they advocate, segregationists must be taken more seriously if they are to be understood. Racist ideas are as rational, systematic, and convincing to segregationists as equalitarian ideas are to integrationists" (p. viii). And I am arguing the further point that in order fully to comprehend the significance of racism we must view it phenomenologically as a passion which has its roots in the fundamental structure of human consciousness. Men do not believe in racism because it is scientifically grounded; they have rather endowed it with scientific credibility *in order* to believe in it.

6. Translated by George J. Becker, New York, Schocken Books, 1948.
7. *Ibid.,* pp. 18–19.
8. *Ibid.,* p. 22.
9. *Ibid.,* pp. 43–45.
10. *The Moral Ambiguity of America,* Ch. V.
11. *New York Review of Books,* August 24, 1967, p. 3.
12. *Ibid.*
13. *The Moral Ambiguity of America,* pp. 64, 85, 19.
14. *Ibid.,* pp. 64–65.
15. *Ibid.,* p. 85.
16. *Ibid.,* pp. 87–88.
17. "The Apocalyptic Temper," *Commentary,* June 1966, p. 66.
18. "A Free Man's Worship," in *Mysticism and Logic,* Anchor Books ed., p. 46.
19. *Pensées,* translated by W. F. Trotter, New York, Random House, 1941, Section VI, No. 347, p. 116.
20. "Concerning Existentialism: A Clarification," *Action,* December 20, 1944, reprinted in *Lettres,* Geneva, 1945, I, 82–88. This is one of Sartre's most lucid explications of the central doctrines of existentialism.
21. Translated by R. A. Audra and C. Brereton, New York, Henry Holt, 1935, p. 306.

CHAPTER SEVEN. THE IMAGINATION OF EVIL
AND THE TRANSCENDENCE OF DESPAIR

1. "Disengagement: The Art of the Beat Generation," p. 352.
2. "Parties and Truth," *Encounter,* April 1957, p. 5.
3. *Pensées,* No. 894, p. 314.

4. "Can We Believe in Judaism Religiously?", *Commentary*, December 1948, p. 524.

5. *Literature and Existentialism*, New York, Citadel, 1962, p. 24.

6. *Saint Genet: Actor and Martyr*, translated by Bernard Frechtman, New York, Braziller, 1963, p. 585.

7. "An Exaltation of Evil," *Saturday Review*, March 11, 1967, pp. 36-37, 113. See also Driver's book, *Jean Genet*, New York, Columbia University Press, 1966.

8. *The Joyful Wisdom*, § 338.

9. If, writes Bergson, mind is to penetrate to the essence of reality, then "it must do itself violence, reverse the direction of the operation by which it ordinarily thinks, continually upsetting its categories, or rather, recasting them. In so doing it will arrive at fluid concepts, capable of following reality in all its windings and of adopting the very movement of the inner life of things. . . . To philosophize means to reverse the normal directions of the workings of thought." "An Introduction to Metaphysics," in *The Creative Mind*, New York, Philosophical Library, 1946, p. 190. See also *Creative Evolution*, New York, Random House, 1944, p. 215.

10. "The White Negro," in *Advertisements for Myself*, New York, G. P. Putnam's Sons, 1959, p. 339, 363.

11. Cited by Diana Trilling in "The Radical Moralism of Norman Mailer," in *The Creative Present*, ed. by N. Balakian and C. Simmons, New York, Doubleday, 1963, p. 168. The essay is reprinted under a slightly different title in Diana Trilling's collection, *The Claremont Essays*, New York, Harcourt, Brace, and World, 1964. See also Granville Hicks's discussion of Mailer in "A Literary Hoax?" (a review of *An American Dream*), *Saturday Review*, March 20, 1965, pp. 23-24.

12. P. 363.

13. Translated by J. B. Baillie, London, Allen and Unwin, 1949, pp. 90-91.

14. *Faust*, Part I, lines 682f. Goethe writes: "Was du ererbt von deinen Vätern hast, Erwirb es, um es zu besitzen! Was man nicht nützt, ist eine schwere Last; Nur was der Augenblick erschafft, das kann er nützen."

15. *The Phenomenology of Mind*, p. 93.

16. *Ibid.*

17. Oxford, Clarendon Press, pp. 227-228.

18. *Ibid.*, p. 226.

19. *Ibid.*, p. 10.

20. *Ibid.*, p. 218.

21. *An Autobiography*, pp. 114-115.

22. *The Idea of History*, p. 85. See also *Speculum Mentis*, pp. 207, 250.

23. *Saturday Review*, March 11, 1967, p. 113.

24. Translated by Maurice Friedman, in *Pointing the Way*, London, Routledge and Kegan Paul, 1957, p. 198.

25. *The Philosophy of Right,* translated by T. M. Knox, Oxford, Clarendon Press, 1945, p. 13.

26. Ronald Gray in "Waiting for Godot," *B.B.C. Listener,* January 24, 1957, pp. 160–161.

27. "The Baal-Shem-Tov's Instruction on Intercourse with God," in *Hasidism and Modern Man,* ed. by Maurice Friedman, New York, Horizon Press, 1958, p. 185.

28. "My Path to Hasidism," in *Hasidism and Modern Man,* p. 59. My italics.

29. Cited by G. Whalley in *Poetic Process,* London, Routledge and Kegan Paul, 1953, p. 104.

30. For this metaphor I am indebted to Lillian Smith's essay "Poets Among Demagogues," *Saturday Review,* October 2, 1965, pp. 24–25.

31. See George P. Grant, *Philosophy in the Mass Age,* Toronto, Copp Clark, 1959, p. 92, and Elizabeth Anscombe, "Modern Moral Philosophy," *Philosophy,* January 1958.

BIBLIOGRAPHICAL NOTE

In addition to the books and articles already cited throughout the main body of the book, as well as in the notes, the following can be recommended as further background reading. No attempt is made here to provide a comprehensive bibliography of works in social pathology; I have simply selected from among a great many works available those which I regard as the most relevant for anyone wishing to pursue the themes discussed in this book.

Robert Ardrey, *African Genesis*, New York, Atheneum, 1961. A playwright defends the unorthodox thesis that man developed from carnivorous, predatory apes, and that his age-old affinity for war, weapons, and aggression is the natural result of this inherited animal instinct. The scientific validity of Ardrey's thesis has been questioned by almost all of his critics. But the book is still worth reading for the imaginative way in which the author comes to grips with the phenomenon of the human condition. In a second book, *The Territorial Imperative* (New York, Atheneum, 1966), Ardrey extends the findings of *African Genesis* to the phenomenon of territorial behavior which he believes to be a product of evolution (rather than a learned phenomenon). Territoriality is represented as the chief mechanism of natural morality, a natural mediating device between the good for one and the good for all. Finally, for an appraisal of Ardrey's views on aggression, see *The Natural History of Aggression,* ed. by J. D. Carthy and F. J. Ebling, New York, Academic Press, 1963.

Daniel J. Boorstin, *The Image,* New York, Atheneum, 1962. An attempt by a distinguished American historian to disclose the illusions that clutter experience and obscure our vision of reality. He argues that Americans have used their wealth, literacy, technology, and progress to create a thicket of unreality. The success of this self-deception, Boorstin writes, is due to the almost pathological "extravagance" of expectation which characterizes the outlook of most Americans.

Norman O. Brown, *Life Against Death,* Middletown, Conn., Wesleyan University Press, 1959. An inquiry into the psychoanalytic meaning of history and culture. Brown's thesis is that mankind must be viewed as largely unaware of its own desires, hostile to life, and unconsciously bent on self-destruction. Freud was right in positing a death instinct, and the development of weapons of destruction makes our present dilemma plain: either we come to terms with our unconscious instincts and drives—with life and with death—or we surely die. A second book, *Love's Body* (New York, Random House, 1966), consists of a series of poetic responses to the main thesis of *Life Against Death.* The survival of man lies in what Brown calls "the way of silence," a new synthesis of mind and body in which the body is recovered and "resurrected" through a "surrender of thought" and "an extinction of the ego."

Geoffrey Clive, *The Romantic Enlightenment,* New York, Meridian Books, 1960. Using several important concepts derived from the thought of Kierkegaard, the author analyzes the ambiguities of Enlightenment thought and the underlying irrationalism which eventually led to its breakdown.

R. G. Collingwood, *The New Leviathan,* Oxford, Clarendon Press, 1942. A study of the rise of absolutism and barbarism in the twentieth century in the light of a new treatise on human nature which brings together the conclusions of a wide variety of the social sciences. A difficult book to read but a highly important contribution to the study of human culture.

Jacques Ellul, *The Technological Society*, New York, Knopf, 1964. A major political theorist studies the threat of technology to individual freedom and looks into the dismal prospects of a society increasingly collectivized, enslaved, and dehumanized by techniques now possible. The main thesis is that technology brings with it inevitable, irreversible collectivist tendencies, regardless of whether society is democratic or totalitarian. In a second book, *Propaganda* (New York, Knopf, 1966), Ellul argues that not only is contemporary man totally enveloped and manipulated by propaganda, but he seems clearly to have embraced it without visible resistance. A third book, *The Political Illusion* (New York, Knopf, 1967), carries the analysis of modern society into the realm of politics and concludes that the overriding malaise of modern civilization is "politization," the permeation of virtually every aspect of life by politics, whether or not there is a political need for it. The solution lies not in "depolitization" but in "repolitization," the rethinking of the role of politics in modern life.

Leslie A. Fiedler, "The New Mutants," *Partisan Review*, Fall 1965. A sympathetic but highly controversial evaluation by a major literary critic of the post-Puritan phenomenon of "non-participation" in society by contemporary youth. The behavior of the new mutants, who prefer meditation to action, suggests the outlines of a new world, a world to be discovered only through the conquest of "inner space" and the extension of "psychic possibility."

Michel Foucault, *Madness and Civilization*, New York, Pantheon Books, 1965. A history of insanity which concentrates on its human and spiritual significance. The author's purpose is not to explain but to understand madness. He thus treats it not as a disease to be handled by a specialist but as a form of life to be entered into. "Then, and then only, can we determine the realm in which the man of madness and the man of reason, moving apart, are not yet distinct . . . and begin the dialogue of their breach, testifying in a fugitive way that they still speak to each other."

Victor E. Frankl, *Man's Search for Meaning*, New York, Washington Square Press, 1963. A moving account of the author's experiences in a concentration camp during World War II.

Erich Fromm, *The Heart of Man: Its Genius for Good or Evil*, New York, Harper and Row, 1965. A lucid statement of Fromm's "normative humanism." The aim of life is the unfolding of man's natural powers; evil is rooted in ignorance and does not stem from man's real nature. To follow evil is therefore to go against one's nature and to destroy oneself as a person. Neurosis is nothing more than a symptom of moral failure, while mental health is a development according to the laws of human nature.

Eugene T. Gendlin, *Experiencing and the Creation of Meaning*, New York, Free Press, 1962. A philosophical and psychological approach to the structure of subjective experience as a source of meaning. The book has important applications to the practice of psychotherapy as well as to the social sciences in general.

Paul Goodman, *People or Personnel*, New York, Random House, 1965. A *cri de coeur* in the grand tradition of humanistic dissent against the dehumanizing tendencies of modern society. "Throughout society," Goodman writes, "the centralizing style of organization has been pushed so far as to become ineffectual, economically wasteful, humanly stultifying, and ruinous to democracy. . . . The only remedy is a strong admixture of decentralization."

Jules Henry, *Culture Against Man*, New York, Random House, 1963. A critique of contemporary American culture, its economy, structure, and values, and the relation of these to national character, parent-child relations, teen-age problems and concerns, the schools, emotional breakdown, old age, and war. The author describes it as a "passionate ethnography" which emphasizes description and interpretation rather than a program of change and reform.

Hans Jonas, *The Phenomenon of Life*, New York, Harper and Row, 1966. An attempt to develop a philosophical anthropology from an existential-phenomenological interpretation of the facts of biology. A work of major importance by a distinguished American philosopher which, although difficult to read, is well worth the effort.

Arthur Koestler, *The Ghost in the Machine*, London, Hutchinson, 1967. A fascinating, nontechnical investigation into the sources of the irrational in Western culture.

Everett Knight, *The Objective Society*, New York, Braziller, 1960. A serious critique of the effects of "scientism" on culture. The author argues that the extension of causality to the whole of human conduct destroys the study of humanity and fosters alienation among those who believe in it. Unless we can relearn to experience our behavior as "intentional," we can never recover our lost sense of humanity.

R. D. Laing, *The Divided Self*, Chicago, Quadrangle Books, 1961. A psychiatrist explores the existential sources of sanity and madness and presents a fresh approach to the problem of alienation. A second book, *The Self and Others* (Chicago, Quadrangle Books, 1962), explores the effects of others on one's own personal experiences and the role of others either in contributing to a person's self-fulfillment or in forcing him to the edge of madness. Laing's most recent book, *The Politics of Experience* (New York, Pantheon, 1967), is an attempt to provide a "self-conscious and self-critical human account of man" which interprets violence as the cry of outraged humanity, and insanity as a retreat from the world of pseudo-events which leads back to one's authentic possibilities. Sometimes it is only by going mad that one can recover one's real self.

Konrad Lorenz, *On Aggression*, New York, Harcourt, Brace and World, 1966. This is perhaps the most widely celebrated and controversial book by a leading naturalist, which traces aggression in both men and animals to an instinctual source and thereby gives some support to Freud's earlier speculations. In this connection see also "The Origins of Human Bonds" by Selma Fraiberg in *Commentary*, December 1967, and Ashley Montagu, *The Human Revolution*, New York, Bantam Books, 1967.

Herbert Marcuse, *Eros and Civilization*, Boston, Beacon Press, 1955. A profound philosophical inquiry into Freud which criticizes Freud's theory of a repressive society in favor of a theory of "non-represssive sublimation." In another book, *One-Dimensional Man* (Boston, Beacon Press, 1964), Marcuse concentrates on the dehumanizing effects of advanced industrial society, which, he argues, has come to function not merely as an instrument for the regulation and realization of human values but as an a priori system or world-view which gives rise to these values. In such a society, the productive apparatus tends to become totalitarian, obliterating the distinction between private and public existence and between technology and politics.

Rollo May, *Man's Search for Himself,* New York, Norton, 1953. An attempt by one of America's leading existential psychoanalysts to develop a theory of man which seeks a way out of despair. Well worth reading and pondering.

B. F. Skinner, *Science and Human Behavior,* New York, Macmillan, 1953. There is no better account of behaviorism and its application to the interpretation of values and to the development of a technology of social control.

George Steiner, *Language and Silence: Essays on Language, Literature and the Inhuman,* New York, Atheneum, 1967. A collection of essays by a brilliant critic who evaluates the whole meaning of humanism in the light of man's inhumane behavior. If the same man can read Goethe at night and then proceed to his job in a concentration camp in the morning, what then of culture?

K. N. Waltz, *Man, the State, and War,* New York, Columbia University Press, 1959. A specialist in international relations considers a number of important questions concerning the relation between human nature and political behavior. The author is particularly concerned with devising a *political* solution to the problem of war, which would serve to control rather than to change human nature.

Rex Warner, *The Cult of Power.* London, Bodley Head, 1946. A collection of essays by the author of *The Professor,* which raises some important questions about the efficacy of the liberal humanist tradition.

Frederick Wertham, *A Sign for Cain: An Explanation of Human Violence,* New York, Macmillan, 1966. A psychiatrist investigates the social and economic sources of violence. He argues that psychological predispositions to violence are learned rather than innate.

Alan Wheelis, *The Quest for Identity*, New York, Norton, 1958. Written by a well-known psychiatrist and psychoanalyst, this is a highly readable and lucid discussion of the conflict between personal identity and the demands of society. Wheelis has also written a highly impressive (and I suspect autobiographical) novel, *The Seeker* (New York, Random House, 1960), which deals with an apparently successful psychoanalyst's inner struggle with nihilism.

In addition to the above I recommend the following issues of *Humanitas* (Journal of the Institute of Man, Duquesne University): Vol. 2, No. 3 (Fall 1966) deals with the theme "Love and Violence," while Vol. 3, No. 3 (Winter 1967) deals with the theme "Dehumanizing Trends in Contemporary Culture." In each case extensive bibliographies are provided. The reader might also consult the Winter 1967 and Spring 1968 issues of the *Partisan Review*, which contain stimulating discussions by several leading American intellectuals of current problems in the United States. The discussions are organized into a symposium around the theme "What's Happening in America?" Finally, I recommend the Summer 1963 number of the *Texas Quarterly*, which has an interesting and substantial symposium on "Individualism in Twentieth-Century America."

INDEX

A NOTE ON THE AUTHOR

Lionel Rubinoff was born in Toronto in 1930 and studied at Queen's University and the University of Toronto, where he received his Ph.D. in philosophy. He has written widely for scholarly journals, and his books include *Faith and Reason, Collingwood and the Reform of Metaphysics,* and a new edition of F. H. Bradley's *Presuppositions of Critical History.* Mr. Rubinoff is now Associate Professor of Philosophy at York University in Toronto, where he lives with his wife and five children.